phrasebooks
and
Paul Geraghty

Fijian phrasebook
2nd edition – July 2008

Published by
Lonely Planet Publications Pty Ltd ABN 36 005 607 983
90 Maribyrnong St, Footscray, Victoria 3011, Australia

Lonely Planet Offices
Australia Locked Bag 1, Footscray, Victoria 3011
USA 150 Linden St, Oakland CA 94607
UK 2nd Floor, 186 City Rd, London EC1V 2NT

Cover illustration
Hibiscus Girl by Ben Johnson

ISBN 978 1 74059 135 5

text © Lonely Planet Publications Pty Ltd 2008
cover illustration © Lonely Planet Publications Pty Ltd 2008

10 9 8 7 6 5 4 3 2

Printed through The Bookmaker International Ltd.
Printed in China

Contents

Introduction

One of the reasons why many visitors from the English-speaking world find Fiji such a congenial place to visit is because they don't have to learn another language: most local people who come into contact with tourists can speak English, and all signs and official forms are also in English.

At the same time, for almost all local people English is not their mother tongue: the majority, the Fijians, speak Fijian at home, while the second largest group, the Indians, speak Fiji Hindi. So, if you really wish to have a more-than-superficial knowledge of the Fijian people and their culture, it is important that you know something of the Fijian language – and, no matter how poor your attempts may be at first, you will be greatly encouraged by the response from your Fijian friends. If you ask for a ticket in English, you will get a ticket. If you ask for a ticket in Fijian, you will get a ticket – and a warm smile of appreciation! Fijians are remarkably tolerant of visitors' attempts to speak their language, and even if you've only managed to string a few words together they will tell you that you speak 'perfect' Fijian. Of course, if you wish to leave the hotels and town centres to visit Fijians in their homes, whether in towns or villages, then some knowledge of Fijian is essential.

Another good reason for acquiring some Fijian is that you have a better chance of being taken for a local by sales personnel, taxi drivers and so on, thus avoiding the 'tourist surcharge' that is often levied on certain services.

Historical Origins

Fiji was probably settled originally some 3500 years ago, and the many regional dialects found in Fiji today all descend, at least partly, from the language spoken by the original inhabitants. They would have come from one of the island groups to the west, either the Solomons or Vanuatu, having left their South-East Asian homeland at least a thousand years previously and spread eastwards by way of Indonesia, the Philippines and Papua New Guinea. From Fiji, groups left to settle the nearby islands of Rotuma, Tonga and Samoa, and from there they spread out to inhabit the rest of Polynesia, from Hawaii in the north to Rapanui (Easter Island) in the east, to Aotearoa (New Zealand) in the south. All of the people in this vast area of settlement speak related languages, belonging to the language family known as 'Austronesian', the most widespread language family in the world. The following table illustrates relationships between a few members of the Austronesian language family.

English	Indonesian, Malay	Nggela, Solomons	Std Fijian	Rotuman	Tongan	Maori
ear	telinga	talinga	daliga	faliga	telinga	taringa
eye	mata	mata	mata	mafa	mata	mata
fish	ikan	iga	ika	i'a	ika	ika
liver	hati	ate	yate	afe	'ate	ate
six	enam	ono	ono	ono	ono	ono
skin	kulit	guli	kuli	'uli	kili	kiri
two	dua	rua	rua	rua	ua	rua

Varieties of Fijian

There are some 300 regional varieties ('dialects') of Fijian, all belonging to one of two major groupings. All varieties spoken to the west of a line extending north-south, with a couple of kinks, across the centre of Vitilevu belong to the Western Fijian group, while all others are Eastern Fijian.

Fortunately for the language learner, there is one variety which is understood by Fijians all over the islands, based on the Eastern varieties of the Bau-Rewa area, which was the major political power centre in the 19th century, before Fiji became a British colony in 1874. This standard form of Fijian is popularly known as 'Bauan' *(vosa vakabau)*, though linguists prefer to reserve this term for the language actually spoken on Bau, and refer to the standard variety as Standard Fijian. It is used in conversation among Fijians from different areas, on the radio and in schools, and is the variety used in this book. Note that in this book we will be focusing on spoken Fijian – the form traditionally used in writing, and in books and newspapers, is slightly different, but the differences are obvious and will present no difficulties. For instance, you will often find *ko* written for *o*, and *ki* or *e* for *i*.

Standard Fijian is not used by Fijians exclusively, but is also known to some extent by members of other communities in Fiji, especially in rural areas. Most Rotumans, Pacific Islanders and part-Europeans

speak it fluently, and many Indians have a working knowledge of it, especially in places like the Sigatoka Valley, Levuka, Savusavu and Taveuni. So Fijian is a useful language to have anywhere in Fiji. Although not officially designated as such, it functions as a national language, and non-Fijians who do speak it are proud of the fact.

Beware of 'Foreigner Talk'!

There is a tradition in Fiji of using a simplified, baby-talk kind of language with non-Fijians, and you should be prepared for it and recognise it. Some of its more conspicuous traits are the incessant use of *sa* and *ko*, lack of prepositions, and so on. For example, the common question *O lako i vei?* 'Where are you going?' becomes *Ko iko sa lako vei?*, and *O kilai au?* 'Do you know me?' becomes *Ko iko sa kila ko yau?* In many cases, you may just have to put up with it, but if the speaker is someone you converse with frequently, you might try asking them to 'speak properly' – *vosa vakadodonu*.

Help!

There are always essential words you need to know in a language. In Fijian, there's the all-purpose greeting: *nī bula* (pronounced 'ni mbula'). For more on this, turn to page 45. 'Yes' is *io* and 'no' is *sega* (senga). Try pages 18 and 19 for more short and easy words for conversation. If you didn't understand or are stuck for words, try page 53. And finally, 'thank you' is *vinaka*; 'thank you very much' is *vinaka vakalevu*; and 'goodbye' is *nī moce* (pronounced 'nee mo-they').

Now you are armed with the essentials, have fun while you learn more, make friends and enjoy your stay in Fiji.

Abbreviations Used in This Book

adj – adjective
f – feminine
inf – informal
intr – intransitive (verb)
m – masculine
n – noun
pl – plural
sg – singular
tr – transitive (verb)
v – verb

Pronunciation

Fijian pronunciation is not especially difficult for the English speaker, since most of the sounds in Fijian are the same as English sounds. The standard Fijian alphabet uses all the English letters, except 'x'. The letters 'h' and 'z' occur only rarely, in borrowed words.

Since the Fijian alphabet was devised relatively recently (in the 1830s), and by a missionary who was also a very competent linguist, it is almost perfectly 'phonetic'. That means that each letter has only one sound, and each sound is represented by only one letter. Once the small number of conventions are learned, Fijian is a dream to pronounce!

Vowels

As with all Pacific languages, the five Fijian vowels are pronounced much as they are in such languages as Spanish, German and Italian:

a	as in 'f**a**ther'
e	as in 'b**e**t'
i	as in 'mach**i**ne'
o	as in 'm**o**re'
u	as in 'z**oo**'

When there are two vowels together, they simply retain their original pronunciation, so that *mai* is pronounced like 'my', *lei* like 'lay', *nau* like 'now', and so on.

Sometimes in this book a vowel will have a line over the top, thus: *ā, ē, ī, ō, ū*. This line over a vowel is known as a 'macron'. It is used in Fijian and other Pacific languages to indicate that the vowel concerned is long – that is, pronounced significantly longer than the same vowel when unmarked. An approximate English equivalent would be the difference between the final vowel sound in 'icy' and 'I see' (note that we're talking about sounds, not spelling – although different letters are used in these two English words, the final sounds are the same, differing only in length).

To get the right pronunciation and meaning of a word, it's important that the length is indicated. For example, *mama* means 'a ring', *mamā* means 'chew it', and *māmā* means 'light (in weight)'. Note that *māmā* takes about twice as long to pronounce as does *mama*. To take another example, *vuvu* means 'muddy, murky', while *vūvū* means 'to have a cough'. There are many more similar examples.

However, Fijians themselves rarely if ever write macrons, since it was not part of the system of writing taught them by the early missionaries, and in any case vowel length is often clear from the context. A parallel situation might be if we were to write English using 'p' for both 'p' and 'b': it would look a little strange, put there would propaply pe very little ampiguity. On the other hand, the macrons are essential for the language learner, and for that reason are used throughout this book.

Consonants

Most consonants are pronounced as they are in English, but a small number of differences need to be learned. First, the minor differences:

b & d pronounced with a preceding nasal consonant, so **b** sounds like 'mb' and **d** like 'nd'

k, p, t as in English, but without the puff of breath that often follows them. The **t** often sounds like 'ch' when it occurs before the vowel **i**, so that *tiko* is often pronounced as if it were *jiko* ('chiko').

r rolled, as in Scottish English, Spanish, etc

v pronounced by placing the lower lip not against the upper teeth, as in English, but against the upper lip.

The following are a little more tricky:

c pronounced as the 'th' in 'this' (not as in 'thick')

g pronounced as the 'ng' in 'sing' (not as in 'angry')

j pronounced as 'ch', but without a following puff of breath

q pronounced as the 'ng' in 'angry' (not as in 'sing')

Here's an alphabetical list of the consonants that differ from English:

b 'mb'

c 'th' as in 'this' (not 'thick')

d 'nd'

g	'ng' as in 'sing' (not 'angry')
j	'ch' without following puff of breath
k	'k' without following puff of breath
p	'p' without following puff of breath
q	'ng' as in 'angry' (not 'sing')
r	rolled
t	't' without following puff of breath, often 'ch' before i
v	with lower lip against upper lip

Occasionally on maps and in tourist publications you'll find a variation on this spelling system which is intended to be easier for English speakers. In this system, Yanuca is spelt 'Yanutha', Beqa 'Mbengga', and so on.

Stress

To 'stress' a vowel means to accent it, that is, to pronounce it so it sounds louder or more prominent than other vowels. For example, in the English word 'education', the 'a' is stressed, the other vowels are not. It is quite easy to know which vowel to stress in Fijian. The rule is, if the final vowel is a long vowel, it is stressed; if not, the one before it is stressed. For example, in both *manā*, 'mangrove lobster', and *Mānā* (name of island), the accent is on the final vowel, but in *mana*, 'effective', it is on the first vowel.

Because the rule is completely regular, there is normally no need to mark stress in Fijian. However, in some long words there is also a secondary stress, that is, a less heavy accent, and this is marked in this book by the use of a bolded letter, thus: *va**l**enivulu* 'classroom'. Note that the last **u** is also stressed, but because this stress is regular it is not marked.

PRONUNCIATION

Intonation

It's difficult to describe intonation in a book such as this, and in most cases the best way to learn is simply to follow the intonation patterns of native speakers. Intonation is important in distinguishing between statements and yes/no questions since, unlike English, word order does not change for questions. Fortunately, the intonation for questions is similar to English, that is, with the pitch of the voice rising towards the end of the sentence. Thus, *kana* with low pitch throughout is an order for someone to eat, whereas *kana?* with high rising pitch is a question meaning 'would you like to eat?'.

Grammar

Fijian is often said to be a relatively easy language to learn, because there are no long lists of verb conjugations, noun declensions, irregular past tenses, and so on. This is true, but Fijian is complex in other departments – as we will see when we turn to the pronouns and possessives – and, although the tense and aspect system is relatively simple, it is difficult for English speakers to master, simply because it has a different basis from that of English.

Learning the grammar of any foreign language is a major undertaking, so be prepared to make a lot of grammatical mistakes as you learn, and always assure your Fijian friends that you want to be corrected, and that you want them to speak to you in proper Fijian *(vakadodonu)* and not in 'foreigner talk': *Vosa vakaviti vakadodonu*, 'Please speak to me in proper Fijian'.

Rerevaka na Kalou ka doka na Tui

17

Most important, don't be *māduā* (timid): keep firing away, and learn from your mistakes. If you drop a real clanger and people laugh at it, have a good laugh with them! Also, remember that to be a good language learner it helps to be a good listener too. Listen to how people say things, and listen to what they say, and use that as a model for what you say and how you say it.

Sentence Structure

Apart from exclamations, all sentences are made up of at least one of two basic elements: 'noun phrases' and 'verb phrases'. Although there are many possible combinations, most sentences consist of either one verb phrase, two noun phrases, or both a noun and a verb phrase. Often the order of elements is different from English, with the verb phrase coming before the noun phrase, so that 'The bus has gone' is often rendered as 'Has gone the bus'. Sentences with two noun phrases (a combination considered ungrammatical in English) will be discussed below under 'To Be'.

Exclamations

These are basically one-word sentences, and are great words to start off learning a language with, because they are in frequent use, and you don't have to learn any grammar! Here are some of the more common ones:

Yes.	*Io.*
No.	*Sega.*
Maybe.	*Dē dua.*
Not yet.	*Se bera.*

GRAMMAR

Note that in answer to a negative question, *io* means the opposite of 'yes' in English. So, for example, if you ask 'don't you know?' *o sega ni kilā?*, the answer *io* means 'I don't know'. Also, the polite way to say 'yes' when someone calls your name is not *io* but *ō*. For 'no', *se bera* should be used if the situation is not final. For example, if a single person is asked whether they are married or not, the reply is *se bera* (even from one with no plans to marry – the expectation in Fijian custom is that all people marry, and an unmarried adult is an object of pity).

GRAMMAR

I see.	*Oi.*
Really.	*Sā dina.*
Wow! Good heavens! etc	*Dou!, Iē!*
How sad! What a pity! How charming! etc	*Isa!*
You must be joking!	*Sā!*
How disgusting!	*Neu!*

Equipped with this battery of reaction words, you can give the impression of understanding every word of a story you're being told. Another very useful interjection is:

| Sorry, what did you say? | *Ō?* |

Remember to use the rising question intonation with this word.

Nouns

There are two major types of noun in Fijian, known as 'common' and 'proper' nouns. All nouns remain unchanged from singular to plural, so, for instance, the word *vale* can mean (one) 'house' or (several) 'houses'.

Common Nouns

Common nouns are all nouns which are not names; that is, they are general words. They are usually preceded by the article *na*:

a/the house, houses	*na vale*
a/the dog, dogs	*na kolī*

As you can see, the one article *na* is both a definite article 'the' and an indefinite article 'a/an'. If 'a/an' means specifically 'one, not more' or 'an unknown one', use *e dua na*:

one house/an (unknown) house	*e dua na vale*

Na is often *a* when it is the first word in a sentence, so the question 'what?' *na cava?* often becomes *a cava?*

Proper Nouns

Proper nouns, which include names of people and places and also independent pronouns and the word for 'who', are usually preceded by the article *o*:

John	*O Jone*
Fiji	*O Viti*
you (sg)	*o iko*
Who?	*O cei?*

Adjectives

Adjectives always follow the noun:

the large house	*na vale levu*
a beautiful house	*na vale totoka*
a dirty shirt	*na sote duka*
the red shirt	*na sote damudamu*

Pronouns

Fijian pronouns present some difficulties to the English speaker because there are more varieties than in English. In number, English has only singular and plural (eg. 'I' and 'we'). Fijian, however, has four number distinctions: singular, dual (for two people), paucal (for a group of people, often a family), and plural (a large number). In addition, there are two words for 'we', 'us', 'our' etc, depending on whether the person you are talking to is included (in which case the 'inclusive' form is used) or not (in which case the 'exclusive' form is used).

GRAMMAR

Independent Pronouns

Let's grab the bull by the horns and have a look at the entire set of independent pronouns:

	singular	dual	paucal	plural
1st person exclusive	*yau*	*keirau*	*keitou*	*keimami*
1st person inclusive	——	*kēdaru*	*kedatou*	*keda*
2nd person	*iko*	*kemudrau*	*kemudou*	*kemunī*
3rd person	*koya*	*rau*	*iratou*	*ira*

The English equivalents of these are:

1st person exclusive	I/me	*yau*
	us two (not you)	*keirau*
	us few (not you)	*keitou*
	us (large number, not you)	*keimami*
1st person inclusive	me and you (sg)	*kēdaru*
	I/we and you (a group)	*kedatou*
	I/we and you (large number)	*keda*
2nd person	you (sg)	*iko*
	you two	*kemudrau*
	you (a group)	*kemudou*
	you (large number)	*kemunī*
3rd person	he/she/it	*koya*
	they two	*rau*
	they (a group)	*iratou*
	they (large number)	*ira*

The 1st person inclusive plural, *keda*, is also commonly used to mean 'one', 'people in general'.

As the name suggests, these independent pronouns are used when the pronoun is uttered by itself, say in answer to the question 'who?', and also when they are the object of a verb. They are very useful for indicating the number of nouns, since nouns themselves do not show number:

the child	*(o koya) na gone*
the two children	*o rau na gone*
the group of children	*o iratou na gone*
the children (large number, or in general)	*o ira na gone*

GRAMMAR

Subject Pronouns

For subjects of verbs, a different set of pronoun forms is used, forms which are generally similar to but shorter than the independent pronouns. The parts in parentheses are often omitted, and must be omitted in imperatives eg. 'Let's go!' (you and me), *Daru lako*!

	singular	dual	paucal	plural
1st person exclusive	*au*	*keirau*	*keitou*	*keimami*
1st person inclusive		*(e)daru*	*(da)tou*	*(e)da*
2nd person	*o*	*(o)drau*	*(o)dou*	*(o)nī*
3rd person	*e*	*(e)rau*	*(e)ratou*	*(e)ra*

Most of the time, we will be using these pronouns in illustrating grammatical points in this chapter. Note that 'he/she/it', *e*, is often omitted, especially before the particle *sā* (see page 31 of this chapter):

He/she/it has gone.   *Sā lako.*

Formal & Informal

Fijian is like most European languages (other than English), in that there are two different ways of saying 'you', 'your', and 'yours' (singular), depending on how you relate to the person you are speaking to. If you are speaking to someone who is your superior, or an adult stranger, you use a longer form (the 'formal' form). This formal form is easy to remember and recognise because it always ends in *nī*. In all other situations, a shorter form (the 'informal' or 'familiar' form) is used.

Throughout this book, these alternatives are indicated either by giving the two sentences, or by putting parentheses round the -*nī* of the formal form. For example:

Where are you from?   *O iko mai vei?* (inf)
                             O kemunī mai vei? (formal)

This means you would say *O kemunī mai vei?* to a superior or adult stranger, otherwise you would use *o iko mai vei?*

How old are you?   *O(nī) yabaki vica?* (formal)

This means you would normally ask *O yabaki vica?*, but to a superior or to an adult stranger you'd say *Onī yabaki vica?*

GRAMMAR

Possession

Possession is another area English speakers find difficult at first, because it is rather more complicated than English. In English there is only one type of possession, for example, there is only one word for 'my'. In Fijian, there are four different ways of saying 'my': *-qu, noqu, kequ, mequ*. Fortunately, the rules are pretty straightforward.

Possessive Pronouns

If the noun is a 'suffix-possessed' noun, which is usually the case with parts of the body, parts of things, and relationship terms, the possessive pronoun is added on to the noun. To illustrate with 'my', *-qu*:

my stomach	*na kete-qu*
my father	*na tama-qu*

If the noun is not suffix-possessed, the following rules apply:

- If I have eaten, or am eating, or will eat the noun, the possessive pronoun is suffixed to *ke-* and comes before the noun:

  my fish (ie the fish that I eat)   *na ke-qu ika*

- If I have drunk, or am drinking, or will drink the noun, the possessive pronoun is suffixed to *me-* and comes before the noun:

  my tea (ie the tea that I drink)   *na me-qu tī*

- In all other cases as, for instance, when I own something or have it in my possession, the possessive pronoun is suffixed to *no-:*

  my house (ie the house that I own or live in)   *na no-qu vale*

The following table gives the complete set of possessive pronoun suffixes used with suffix-possessed nouns:

	singular	dual	paucal	plural
1st person exclusive	*qu*	*ikeirau*	*ikeitou*	*ikeimami*
1st person inclusive	—	*daru*	*datou*	*da*
2nd person	*mu*	*mudrau*	*mudou*	*munī*
3rd person	*na*	*drau*	*dratou*	*dra*

The possessive pronoun suffixes used with *ke-*, *me-*, and *no-* are the same as the above, except for the 1st person exclusive, where the *-ike-* is omitted. So 'our (dual: 1st person exclusive) father' is *tama-ikeirau* but 'our (dual: 1st person exclusive) tea' is *na me-irau tī*. Note also that *no-* becomes *ne-* in these non-singular exclusive forms: *ne-irau*, *ne-itou*, *ne-imami*.

With Proper Nouns

If the possessor is a proper noun, the forms *i*, *kei*, *mei* and *nei* are used:

Peter's father	*na tama i Pita*
Mary's stomach	*na kete i Mere*
Timothy's fish	*na ika kei Timoci*
Ruth's tea	*na tī mei Ruci*
Paul's house	*na vale nei Paula*

Note the following order with adjectives:

Paul's large house	*na vale levu nei Paula*

Verbs

Verbs are relatively regular in Fijian, and can be classed into four major types.

Simple Verbs

A 'simple' verb is one that is never used with a direct object and so never changes its form. (With the next two verb types you'll see what a direct object is and how it works with a verb.) Examples of simple verbs are *gādē* 'go for a walk, go on holiday etc' and *māduā* 'be ashamed':

I'm on holiday.	*Au gādē.*
He's ashamed.	*E māduā.*

Active Transitive Verbs

An 'active transitive' verb is similar to a simple verb, but a suffix consisting of a consonant plus -*a* (or sometimes just -*a*) is added when the verb has a direct object. A direct object is something that is directly affected by the verb. An example of an 'active transitive' verb is the word for 'drink', *gunu-va*. The direct objects here are 'it' (what is being drunk) and 'the tea' (also being drunk):

I'm drinking.	*Au gunu.*
I'm drinking it.	*Au gunuva.*
I'm drinking the tea.	*Au gunuva na tī.*

Note also the following construction:

I'm drinking tea.	*Au gunu tī.*

Passive Transitive Verbs

A 'passive transitive' verb is one which also has a suffix added when the verb has a direct object, but which has a *passive* meaning when the verb is used without the suffix.

An example of a 'passive transitive' verb is the word for 'close', *sogo-ta*. In these examples, the first phrase has an active sense (I closed it) while the second phrase is passive as the verb simply explains an existing state (it's just sitting there, closed).

I closed the shop.	*Au sogota na sitoa.*
The shop is closed.	*E sogo na sitoa.*

Transitive Only Verbs

The final class of verbs is those which are *only* used transitively, so always have a transitive suffix attached to them. An example is the word for 'remember', *nanuma*:

I remember your face.	*Au nanuma na matamu.*

The final -*a* of the suffix of *all* transitive verbs changes to -*i* when followed by an object that is a proper noun or independent pronoun:

I remember you. (sg)	*Au nanumi iko.*

Do you remember Charlie?	*O nanumi Jale?*
I'm afraid of him/her.	*Au rerevaki koya.*

Note that if a transitive verb ends in -*ā*, the form before a proper noun or independent pronoun object is -*ai*:

Do you know the house?	*O kilā na vale?*
Do you know us (group)?	*O kilai keitou?*

So What Verb is That?

Remember the simple verb never needs to change and it doesn't have an object. 'I'm on holiday', 'they're on holiday', 'I'm going for a walk', 'you're going for a walk', and so on.

There's no sure way to tell whether a particular transitive verb has the 'active' or 'passive' sense when used without a suffix, but the meaning often helps. Most verbs that indicate a process done by a person to a thing are 'passive transitives', eg. 'to paint' *boro-ya* ('It's been painted', *sā boro*);'to cut' *koti-va* ('the paper is cut, *sā koti na pepa*)'; 'to open' *dola-va* ('the door is open' *e dola na kātuba*); 'to break open' *basu-ka*; 'to carry' *kau-ta*, and so on.

Verbs of emotion ('afraid of' *rere-vaka*), motion ('ascend' *cabe-ta*), and saying ('to deny' *caki-taka*) tend to be 'active transitives'.

Particles

Particles are short words that come before or after the verb and modify its meaning. In other words, they do much of the work of modal verbs, adverbs and tenses in English. We will look at some of the more common particles, beginning with those that occur before the verb (but after the subject pronoun).

Tense

Tense (that is, the past, present and future) is indicated by particles straight after the subject pronoun.

The use of tense is optional in Fijian (unlike English), which means that if it's obvious to the listener that you're relating an episode that happened last week, there's no need for any particle to indicate tense. If you do want to show tense, the past is *ā*, and the future is *na*:

I went.	*Au ā lako.*
I will go.	*Au na lako.*

Particles *sā* & *se*: There is a kind of tense that has no direct equivalent in English, and it's indicated by the particles *sā* and *se*. The particle *sā* is used when the event is a new development, a change from a previous state, whereas its opposite *se* indicates that the event is not new, but continues a previous state. So *sā* may be used to translate 'now' (but not previously), or 'have' (a development in the recent past), or 'about to' (a recent development in the immediate future):

My child is (now) at school.	*Sā vuli na luvequ.*
We (group) have eaten.	*Keitou sā kana.*
I'm going. (ie I'm about to go)	*Au sā lako.*

On the other hand, *se* translates as 'still':

My child is (still) at school.	*Se vuli na luvequ.*
We (group) are still eating.	*Keitou se kana.*

Particle *qai*: By itself, *qai* means 'then, next'; after *sā* it means 'at last, finally'; and after *se* it means 'just now, recently, just previously':

Then we (group) got on board.	*Keitou qai vodo.*
He/she's finally gone to sleep.	*Sā qai moce.*
No thanks, I've just eaten.	*Vinaka, au se qai kana (oti).*

Other Preverbal Particles

Apart from those that mark tense, the most common particles occurring before the verb are:

always, habitually, alot (often used to translate the simple present tense)	*dau*
too	*rui*
want to	*via*
come and	*mai*
go and	*lai*

Do you smoke?	*O(nī) dau vakatavako?*
We (large number) play alot.	*Keimami dau qito.*
I'm too thin.	*Au rui lila.*
Do you (two) want to play cards?	*Drau via veimau?*
Come and have a drink!	*Mai gunu!*
Afterwards go and swim in the sea.	*Oti lai sili waitui.*

Postverbal Particles

The following are some of the more common particles occurring after the verb. Note that when two or more are used, they occur in the order as they are listed here:

up	*cake*
down	*sobu*
away	*tani*
already (with *sā* before the verb, translates the perfect tense)	*oti*
really	*dina*
all	*kece*
immediately, right now, very	*sara*
again	*tale*
continuous tense	*tiko*
maybe, might	*beka*
please, if you don't mind	*mada*
only, just	*gā*
here, towards me	*mai*
there, towards you	*yani*
there, in it, on it, with it etc	*kina*

Bring it up to me.	*Kauta cake mai.*
I'm about to go down to you.	*Au sā lako sobu yani.*
Go away right now! (to a group)	*Dou lako tani sara!*
I've already seen it.	*Au sā raica oti.*

Do you really know?	*O kilā dina?*
We (group) have all eaten.	*Keitou sā kana oti kece.*
It's very fast.	*E totolo sara.*
I'll play cards again.	*Au na veimau tale.*
The children are playing.	*Era qito tiko na gone.*
It might be closed.	*Sā sogo beka.*
Please look for it.	*Vāqarā mada.*
May I see it?	*Au raica mada.* (lit. I see it please)
I'm only joking.	*Au veiwali gā*
Please look this way.	*Rai mada mai.*
I'll give you a call (phone).	*Au na qīri yani.*
They're playing there.	*Era qito tiko kina.*

To Be

There is no direct equivalent of the verb 'to be'.

- If the meaning is 'be one of a class, profession etc', no verb is used, but the noun rather functions as a verb:

I am a doctor.	*Au vuniwai.*
They might be schoolchildren.	*Era gonevuli beka.*
We are all human.	*Eda tamata kece.*

- If the meaning is 'to be located' or 'to exist', a number of verbs may be used, but the most common are *tiko* and *tū*; *tū* implies a more permanent location or existence:

I will be there tomorrow.	*Au na tiko kina nimataka.*
They (group) are still outside.	*Eratou se tiko i tuba.*

| Is there any sugar? | *E tiko na suka?* |
| Are there roads there? | *E tū kina na gaunisala?* |

- The expression 'been to', meaning 'gone to and come back', is translated by *lesu mai* (lit 'return from'):

| Have you been to Australia? | *O sā lesu mai Ositerēlia?* |

To Have

There is no direct equivalent of 'to have'.

- The most common equivalent is to use *(e) dua* plus a possessive construction:

| Do you have a pen? | *E dua nomu(nī) peni?* |
| He/She has a house now. | *Sā dua nona vale.* |

- With certain more permanent and substantial possessions, simply prefix *vaka* to the noun and use it as a verb:

They all have houses.	*Era vakavale kece.*
I have a gun.	*Au vakadakai.*
Are you married? (ie do you have a husband/ wife?)	*O vakawati?*

Note that *vaka* becomes *vā* before a word beginning with *k*, *q*, or *g*:

| He has a beard. | *E vākumi.* |
| Do you (family) have a dog? | *Dou vākolī?* |

Questions

Yes/no questions are marked by a rising intonation. Other question words are:

what	*cava*
who	*cei*
where	*vei*
how	*vakacava*
how much/many	*vica*
when	*naica*
when (at what time)?	*ina vica*

What do you want?	*A cava o(nī) vinakata?*
Who said so?	*O cei ā kaya?*
Where's Michael?	*I vei o Maikeli?*
How did you two meet?	*Drau sota vakacava?*
How many children do you have now?	*Sā vica na luvemu?*
When did you (group) arrive?	*Dou yaco mai naica?*
What time will it close?	*E na sogo ina vica?*

For 'why' as a single word question, use *baleta*. For 'why' in a sentence, use *(a) cava ... kina*, the equivalent of 'what for?':

Why?	*Baleta?*
Why do you want to go?	*Cava o via lako kina?*

Negatives

The negative is formed by *sega ni* (often sounding like *seni* in rapid speech). It occurs after the subject pronoun and tense particles, but before the other particles:

I don't know.	*Au sega ni kilā.*
They don't want to lie down.	*Era sega ni via davo.*
I'm not going to school now.	*Au sā sega ni vuli.*
(I've left school)	
Didn't you go swimming?	*O ā sega ni lai sili?*
I'm not happy.	*Au sā sega ni mārau.*

Imperative

The imperative is, as in English, the simple form of the verb. But remember that this is valid only for the singular – for numbers other than the singular, the appropriate subject pronoun should be used:

Go on!	*Lako!*
Shut up! (the two of you)	*Drau tikolō!*
Eat! (to group or family)	*Dou kana!*

The negative imperative is *kua ni*:

Don't tell lies!	*Kua ni lasu!*

Modals
Can

The English 'can' is translated by *rawa ni* after the subject pronoun:

Can you walk?	*O(nī) rawa ni taubale?*

GRAMMAR

Should/Ought To

For 'should' and 'ought to', use *dodonu me*:

It ought to be open.   *E dodonu me dola.*

May/Might

For 'may' and 'might', use the postverbal particle *beka*:

It may be open.   *E dola beka.*

Must/Have To

For 'must', there is no single translation. When it means 'obliged to', use the conjunction *me/mo*:

You must be there at two.   *Mo tiko kina ina rua.*

When it means 'probably', use *rairai* before the verb:

I must have made a mistake.   *Au rairai cala.*

For 'must not', use *kua ni* or the verb *tabu*:

I mustn't be late.   *Meu kua ni bera.*
You mustn't touch it.   *Mo kua ni tarā.*
One mustn't touch it.   *E tabu ma tarā.*

Want To

For 'want to', use the preverbal particle *via*:

Do you want to dance?   *O via dānisi?*

Comparatives & Superlatives

Often the meaning is already clear in the sentence, or the postverbal particle *cake* may be used.

He/she/it's better.	*E vinaka cake.*
I'm looking for a larger house.	*Au vāqarā e dua na vale levu (cake).*
I'm much faster than you.	*Au totolo sara vei iko.*
Who's the older of you two?	*O cei e qase vei kemudrau?*

Superlatives are formed by placing *duadua* after the adjective:

The largest kava bowl.	*Na tānoa levu duadua.*

Prepositions

There are only four commonly used prepositions, ie words that mean 'in, at, to, from, with, about, etc':

i	used with things and places
mai	used with distant things and places
vei	used with people (including pronouns). *Vei* is joined with the third person singular (he/she) as *vuā*.
kei	means '(together) with'

I'm staying in Suva.	*Au tiko i Suva.*
Go away from here.	*Lako tani i kē.*
They come from New Zealand.	*Era lako mai Niusiladi.*

Go to Peter.	*Lako vei Pita.*
Go to him/her.	*Lako vuā.*
I'm staying with Margaret.	*Au tiko vei Makareta.*
(ie. at her place)	
I'm talking with my father.	*Keirau veivosaki kei tamaqu.*

Notice that the pronoun form in the last example (us two) includes myself and my father as subjects.

To be more specific about location, use words such as:

top	*dela-*
underneath	*ruku-*
side	*yasa-*
inside	*loma-*
front	*mata-*
back, behind	*daku-*

It's on top of the table.	*E tiko e dela ni tēveli.*
Enter from that side.	*Curu mai yasana yā.*
Watch out! Behind you!	*Qarauna! I dakumu!*

Much of the work of English prepositions is carried out by transitive suffixes to verbs, eg. 'angry' *cudru*, 'angry with' *cudru-va*; 'think' *vākāsama*, 'think about' *vākāsama-taka*:

Don't be angry with me.	*Kua ni cudru-vi au.*
Let's (you and I) think about it.	*Daru vākāsama-taka.*

Conjunctions

Conjunctions are words that join shorter sentences to form longer ones. The most common Fijian conjunctions are:

that, when, because	*ni*
so that (but 'so that you' is *mo)*	*me*
or	*se*
if	*kē(vakā)*
in case, lest, might	*dē*

I know that it's closed.	*Au kilā ni sā sogo.*
He/she was surprised when he/she saw me.	*E kurabui ni raici au.*
Sleep so you can wake early in the morning.	*Moce mo yadra vakamataka.*
Are you going or not?	*O lako se sega?*
If there's room on the bus we'll (you and I) take it.	*Kē galala na basi daru vodo.*
It might rain/In case it rains.	*Dē tau na uca.*

Demonstratives

In English there are two types of demonstratives, close to the speaker (this/these, here) and distant (this/those, there). In Fijian there are three, close to the speaker, close to the hearer, and distant. The forms used are:

this	qō
that (close to speaker)	qori
that (distant)	yā
here	kē
there (close to speaker)	keri
there (distant)	keā

This house.	*Na vale qō.*
That pen (you have).	*Na peni qori.*
That village (over there).	*Na koro yā.*
Just stay here.	*Tiko gā i kē.*
Wait where you are.	*Wāwā i keri.*
Please look over there.	*Rai mada i keā.*

A common way of using demonstratives is with *vā* 'like': *vāqō* 'like this', *vāqori* 'like that (like you're doing)', *vāyā* 'like that':

I did it like this/this way.	*Au cakava vāqō.*
Don't be like that!	*Kua ni vāqori!*
That's the way it is.	*Sā vāyā.*

Making Your Own Sentences

Remember when making your own sentences that very often (though not always) the verb phrase comes first in the sentence. There are no hard and fast rules, and as always the best way to learn is to listen and imitate. Try reading the phrases in the book and attempt to substitute other nouns, verbs, and so on, so as to create your own sentences.

Greetings & Civilities

Using the appropriate greetings and civilities in Fijian can be quite complicated, because there are more than in English. However, there are a small number of basic ones that will get you by.

Greetings

Introductions are not necessary, but the following expressions may be used:

May I introduce you to ...?	*Drau sota mada kei ...*
Shake hands with ...	*Drau lūlulu kei ...*
This is ...	*Qō o ...*

If there is no-one to do the introductions:

Let's shake hands (you and I).	*Daru lūlulu mada.*
My name is ...	*O yau o ...* (lit. I am ...)
I'm from ...	*O yau mai ...*

Shaking hands was introduced to Fiji in the 19th century by way of Tonga (the word for it *lūlulu* is borrowed from the Tongan *lulululu*) and quickly became the established custom. An affectionate handshake can be very long, and even last throughout the entire conversation. When introduced to a high chief, it's the Fijian custom to sit or crouch down immediately after the handshake, bow the head, and *cobo* (clap with hollowed hands) three or more times. This is not required for non-Fijians.

44

The all-purpose greeting, as you no doubt already realise if you are visiting Fiji, is *bula* (lit 'live'), which corresponds to 'hello', 'pleased to meet you', 'how are you?' etc. Remember to use the appropriate pronoun number if required (see page 23):

Hello! (to two people)   *Drau bula!*
Hello! (to a group of people)   *Dou bula!*
Hello! (to a large number of   *Nī bula!*
people, or to a superior or
adult stranger)

In reply, you may either simply say *io* or *ia* (a bit more respectful), or return the *bula*, or both *(io, bula!* etc).

If it is morning, use *yadra* (lit 'wake') rather than *bula* as a greeting. As with *bula*, the reply is to simply say *io* or *ia* (a bit more respectful), or return the *yadra*, or both *(io, yadra!* etc).

Greetings when Passing

When passing someone in the road or village, you should always greet them. A smile and a nod and a *io* will do, but a fuller greeting (*bula* or *yadra*, as described above) is nicer, and you should always remember the appropriate pronoun number. After the greeting, it is customary to enquire as to each other's movements:

Where are you going?   *O(nī) lai vei?*

Or, if you know that they are on their way home:

Where have you been?   *O(nī) lesu mai vei?*

Such questions may sound rude in English to some, but in Fiji they are the custom. It's perfectly in order to give a very vague reply:

I'm just going in this direction.	*(Au) se lako* or *(Gole) mada vāqō.*
I'm going to see something over here.	*(Au) se rai mada i kē.*
Nowhere in particular, just back from over there.	*Sega, lesu gā mai keā.*
Nowhere special, just going for a walk.	*Sega, gādē gā.*

But if you wish to be more specific:

I'm going ...	*Au se lako mada ...*
home	*i vale/neitou*
to the village	*i na koro*
to the hotel	*i na ōtela*
to the shop	*i na sitoa*
to the bank	*i na baqe*
to the post office	*i na posi*

GREETINGS

to the restaurant/dining-room	*i valenikana*
to the school	*i koronivuli*
to the church	*i valenilotu*
to work	*i cakacaka*
to eat	*i kana*
to bed	*i moce*
for a swim in the sea	*i sili waitui*
to Suva	*i Suva*
to see Mere	*vei Mere*

Remember that the *se* and *mada* are for politeness, and may be omitted, such as when you pass a friend; and that *gole* is often used instead of *lako*.

For 'coming from' use *lesu mai na baqe* (I'm coming from the bank), *lesu mai koronivuli* (I'm coming from school), *lesu mai vei Mere* (I'm coming from visiting Mary), etc.

When someone has told you where they're going or coming from, say *vinaka* (thanks), and say where you're going to or coming from, if you haven't already done so, then say 'goodbye' (next section).

If you are passing in a hurry or at a distance, smile and nod and point in the direction you are going.

Leaving

If you have to leave briefly but intend to return, say *au se lako au qai lesu tale mai* (I'm going for a bit but I'll be back), or *au na lesu tale mai* (I'll be back).

To wrap up a conversation, say something like *ia sā vinaka* (well thanks) or *sa i koya* (that's it). Next, state that you wish to leave: *au se lako/gole mada*, perhaps adding where you are going

GREETINGS

(as in preceding section). A very polite way of saying 'I wish to leave' is *au sā tatau meu sā lako* or *au sā tatau meu sā lesu tale* (*tatau* means 'to take leave'). The reply is a word of thanks such as *vinaka*, *io vinaka*, *sā vinaka*, *vinaka vakalevu*.

If you are leaving someone's home, they will probably invite you to stay for the next meal before you leave:

Please stay for breakfast/lunch/dinner.	*Tou katalau/vakasigalevu/vakayakavi mada.*
Please stay for a cup of tea.	*Tou gunu tī mada.*
The breakfast/lunch/dinner isn't ready yet.	*(Se) bera tiko na katalau/vakasigalevu/vakayakavi.*

If you wish to decline politely, again use a word of thanks such as *vinaka*.

The all-purpose word of farewell is *moce* (literally 'sleep'), again with the appropriate pronoun if required; *mada* may be added for politeness, eg. *dou moce mada* (to a group or family). As with *bula* and *yadra*, the reply is to simply say *io* or *ia* (a bit more respectful), or return the *moce*, or both *(io, moce!* etc).

Announcing your departure and saying *moce* is only correct if you will not see that person again for a while. If you expect to meet the person again soon, you should say something like:

See you later.	*Au sā liu mada.* (lit 'I'm going on ahead')
	Qai muri yani? (lit 'Will you follow me?')

To which the reply is *io* 'yes', and possibly:

I'll join you later.	*Au na qai muri yani.*

The word *moce* is also appropriate, and commonly used, as a greeting to a stranger you pass in the evening or at night, or shouted to people passing in vehicles on their way to distant parts (at any time of the day).

Finally, you may wish to send your regards or love with your departing guest. *Loloma yani* is the general expression; to specify, add *vei* ...

Give my regards to Joe.	*Loloma yani vei Jo.*
Give my love to your wife and kids.	*Loloma yani vei iratou na veitinani.*

Civilities

The usual word for thanks, appreciation, congratulations, etc is *vinaka* or, more profusely, *vinaka vakalevu* or *vinaka sara vakalevu*. In response to an invitation, however, *vinaka* usually means 'no thanks'. If you wish to accept, do so with a smile and then say *vinaka*.

Any time you see someone while you are eating, it is customary to invite them to eat with you. If eating sweets, biscuits, fruit, or snacks, or smoking cigarettes, just hand over the packet, bunch of bananas etc, perhaps saying *qori*, 'there you are'. To say something like 'you can have one' is considered ridiculously mean; even asking *kana?* or *dua na kemu?*, 'would you like one?', might suggest you are sharing reluctantly.

If eating at table in a restaurant or at home, use an appropriate gesture or call. The bare minimum is to point at the food and look inquiringly. In increasing order of politeness, use *(mai) kana, (mai) kana mada, nī (mai) kana mada*. The word *mai* means 'come and', so is more appropriate when calling to someone some distance away.

To decline such an invitation, use a word of thanks *(vinaka, etc)*, and say or point to where you are going (preceding section). In familiar situations, the minimum is to cock the head, meaning 'no thanks', and pat the stomach to show it's full.

Grace is always said before meals. During meals, the host may say:

Eat heartily.	*Kana vakavinaka.*
Eat a lot.	*Kana vakalevu.*
[a chiding at you for eating too little]	*O(nī) kana vakalailai!*

When you've had enough:

Thanks a lot for the food, please may I retire?	*Vinaka vakalevu na kākana, au sā kere vakacegu.*
Have you had enough?	*O(nī) sā mamau?*
I've had enough, thankyou.	*Au sā mamau, vinaka vakalevu.*

To all who pass when people are drinking kava, it is customary to call *mai dua na bilo!* (come and have a cup!). If someone sneezes, say *bula!*; if they sneeze again, *tubu!* (grow!) or *moli!* (health!). They may thank you by saying *moli* once or a few times.

Forms of Address

Fijians usually have two names, a Christian name followed by a traditional name. One of these will be used as the common form of address. Some have also adopted the practice of having a family surname, using the father's traditional name. In some places, especially parts of the main island of Vitilevu, it is polite to call a married man *tamai ...* (father of ...) and a married woman *tinai ...* (mother of ...), using the name of their oldest child.

People of standing in the community are often addressed by their office or their partner's office:

Good morning ...	*(Nī) yadra ...*
teacher	*qasenivuli*
minister (of religion)	*na (tūraga) italatala*
minister's wife	*radini (talatala)*
doctor	*vuniwai*
doctor's wife	*rādinivuniwai*

The word *radini* may also be used for the wife of any dignitary.

GREETINGS

Attracting Someone's Attention

To attract from a distance the attention of a friend, child, taxi driver etc, a loud sudden hiss seems to penetrate any noise. The beckoning gesture is to wave with the palm downwards.

Come here!	*Mai!*
[to attract the attention of an adult stranger]	*Kemunī!*
I wonder if I might bother you.	*Au kerekere mada.*

To attract the attention of someone sitting next to you, it is customary to tap or scratch lightly a couple of times on their thigh. This can be a little alarming the first time it happens to you, so be prepared.

To express appreciation of the opposite sex and inquire into the possibility of further acquaintance, the most common of a large number of expressions is (at time of going to press!) *bā rewa*. The etymology of this expression has been the subject of much debate, but it most likely derives from a Western Fijian phrase meaning 'might it be possible?'. If you wish to respond or, as is frequently the case, carry on the joke, say *bā rewa gā vei iko* or *i keri gā* (same to you).

Apologies & Requests

A general word of apology, for keeping someone waiting, treading on someone's foot, knocking into someone in the street, etc, is *(nī) vosota sara*, or *(nī) vosoti au*. This may be preceded by an expression of annoyance with oneself and/or pity such as *oilei* or *isa*. If there is time to reply, say *sega ni dua na kā* (it's nothing), or just *sega*. There is no need to apologise for belching.

There is a special word of apology, *tilou* or *jilou*, which is used, often repeatedly, when you have to 'invade someone's space', as defined in Fijian culture. Examples are pushing your way through a crowd (eg. when getting off a bus), touching a part of someone's body (especially the head), passing behind or in front of someone sitting down, or standing up in a house when people are sitting down. If you have to stand up in a house – to get something from a shelf, take down the lamp to pump it, or some such thing – first request permission *(au se tarā mada na ...)*, then when you sit down again *cobo* (clap with hollowed hands) a few times.

The normal way to broach a request is *au kerekere mada*. If it is a particularly difficult request, begin with *(nī) yalovinaka* (be kind). For instance, if you wish to ask a stranger not to smoke, it would be extremely rude to put the request directly, so say something like: *I kemunī, nī yalovinaka, e dau lako vakacā vei au na tavako* (excuse me, be kind, I'm allergic to tobacco).

Pardon (what did you say?)	*Ō?*
Please say that again more slowly.	*Tukuna tale mada vakamālua.*
More slowly please.	*Vakamālua mada.*
I didn't get that.	*Au sega ni taura rawa.*
May I ...?	*Au ... mada?*
Excuse me. (may I go past you)	*Au lako mada yani.*
Sure. (you may go past me)	*Mai!*
Sorry. (general)	*(Nī) vosota sara* or *(Nī) vosoti au.*
Sorry. (if invading space)	*Tilou/Jilou.*
It's nothing.	*Sega ni dua na kā.*

Body Language & Etiquette

The headshake means 'no', as in English; 'yes' is more an upward nod of the head and/or raising the eyebrows. Generally speaking, Fijians are not a demonstrative people.

When in a Fijian cultural situation, especially a village, be as quiet as possible. Dress conservatively. Going to or from bathing, do not drape your towel over your shoulder. As soon as you enter a house, sit down on the floor. When told to move to another place in the house, crawl there, remembering to say *jilou* as you pass people.

If you are invited to a *yaqona* (kava) drinking session, remember that seating is governed by seniority and rank, so just sit where you are told; in particular, don't go and sit in front of the *tānoa* (kava bowl) unless you are told to do so. *Yaqona* is served in rounds. When you are offered a bowl of *yaqona*, clap with cupped hands *(cobo)* two or three times, take the cup and drink its

contents in one go. Return the cup and *cobo* again. After others have drunk you may *cobo* and/or say *maca!* (the cup is empty). If you are among friends and feel it's time for the next round, say *taki* or *talo*. If you wish to stop drinking, extend the palm of your hand outwards in front of you when your cup comes and say *au sā kua mada* or *au sā cegu mada*. If you wish to stretch your legs, request permission by saying *au se dodo mada*.

GREETINGS

Small Talk

Having been introduced or having introduced yourself, you may want to get better acquainted with your Fijian friend. Here are some suitable topics for your conversation.

Meeting People

What is your name?	*O cei na yacamu(nī)?*
My name is ...	*O yau* (or *Na yacaqu*) *o ...*
Pleased to meet you.	*Ia, (nī) bula.*

If you would like to 'Fijianise' your given name, here are some of the most common equivalents:

John	*Jone*
Mary	*Mere*
Peter	*Pita*
Jane	*Seini*
Paul	*Paula*
Elizabeth	*Ilisāpeci*
Timothy	*Tīmoci*
Margaret	*Makareta*

Nationalities

Fijians are often very curious about a person's nationality, and enjoy hearing about other countries.

Where are you from?	*O iko/kemunī mai vei?*

56

I am from ...	*O yau mai ...*
Australia	*Ositerēlia*
Canada	*Kenatā*
England	*Igiladi*
Europe	*Urope*
France	*Farānisē*
Germany	*Jāmani*
India	*Idia*
Ireland	*Aeladi*
Japan	*Jāpani*
Korea	*Korea*
the Middle East	*Ēsia i loma*
New Zealand	*Niusiladi*
Norway	*Nōwei*
Samoa	*Sāmoa*
Scotland	*Sikoteladi*
Sweden	*Suiteni*
Tonga	*Toga*
the USA	*Merika*
Wales	*Wēlesi*

Age

Age is not a taboo subject in Fiji, so don't be surprised or offended if people ask your age. Birthdays are not normally celebrated, and quite a few Fijians neither know nor care on what day they were born.

How old are you?	*O(nī) yabaki vica?*
I am … years old.	*Au yabaki …*
18	*tinikawalu*
25	*ruasagavulukalima*

See the Numbers chapter (page 134) for your particular age.

Occupations

What do you do (for a living)?	*A cava na nomu(nī) cakacaka?*
I am a/an …	*Au …*
accountant	*daunifika*
actor	*ekta*
artist	*daudroini*
bartender	*bāmeni*
builder	*mātai*
bus driver	*draiva ni basi*
business person	*daunibisinisi*
carpenter	*mātai*
dockworker	*cakacaka ena wavu*
doctor	*vuniwai*
engineer	*idinia*

factory worker	*daubuliyāyā*
farmer	*dauteitei*
journalist	*dauvolaitukutuku*
labourer	*leiba*
lawyer	*loya*
mechanic	*mekeniki*
merchant	*vakasitoa*
minister (church)	*italatala*
musician (instrumentalist)	*dauqiriqiri, dauvakatagi*
nurse	*nasi*
office worker/clerk	*vunivola*
plumber	*palama*
police officer	*ovisa*
politician	*daunipolitiki*
postal worker	*daukaumeli*
researcher	*dauvakadidike*
sailor/mariner	*dausoko*
scientist	*saentisi*
secretary	*vunivola*
shop assistant	*dauvolivolitaki*
singer	*daulagasere*
soldier	*sōtia*
student	*gonevuli*
taxi driver	*draiva ni teksi*
teacher	*qasenivuli*
villager	*tū vakavanua*
waiter (f)	*weitres*
waiter (m)	*weita*
writer	*dauvolaivola*

Religion

Fijians are not at all embarassed about asking someone what their religion is. Almost all Fijians are Christians, about 75% being Methodist and 14% Catholic.

What is your religion?	*O(nī) lotu cava?*
I am ...	*Au ...*
Assemblies of God, etc	*lotu qiriqiri, lotu asembli*
Buddhist	*lotu Buda*
Catholic	*(lotu) Katolika*
Christian	*lotu Vākarisitō*
Church of England,	*lotu Jaji*
Episcopal	
Hindu	*lotu Idū*

Jehovah's Witness	*lotu Vakadinadina*
Jewish	*lotu Jiu*
Methodist	*(lotu) Waiselē*
Mormon	*lotu Mōmani*
Muslim	*lotu Musulimi/Musolomani*
not religious	*sega ni lotu*
Seventh Day Adventist	*lotu Kavitu*

Family

Fijians are interested in one's status within the family, so you should not be surprised or offended by such questions.

Are you married?	*O(nī) vakawati?*
No I'm not.	*Se bera.*
I am single.	*Au sega ni vakawati.*
How many children do you have?	*Lē vica na luvemu(nī)?*
I don't have any children.	*E sega na luvequ.*
I have a daughter/son.	*E dua na luvequ yalewa/tagane.*
How many brothers/sisters do you have?	*Kemudou lē vica na veitacini?* (lit: how many are you?, so include yourself in the reply)
How many boys/girls?	*Lē vica na tagane/yalewa?*
There are two boys and three girls in our family.	*Keitou lē rua na tagane, lē tolu na yalewa.*
Where do you come in the family?	*O(nī) kavica (ni qase)?*
I'm the oldest.	*Au ulumatua.*

I'm the second oldest.	*Au karua (ni qase).*
I'm the youngest.	*Au kena itini.*
Is your husband/wife here?	*Drau lako mai vakaveiwatini?*
Do you have a boyfriend/ girlfriend?	*E dua nomu(nī) itau (tagane/yalewa)?*

Relations

All the words below are listed in the first person possessive (my aunt, my brother, etc). See the section on Possession in the Grammar chapter (page 25) for possessives other than 'my'.

my ...

aunt (father's sister)	*no-qu nei*
aunt (mother's older sister)	*tina-qu levu* or *no-qu nā levu*
aunt (mother's younger sister)	*tina-qu lailai* or *no-qu nā lailai*
brother (female speaking)	*gāne-qu*
older brother (male speaking)	*tuaka-qu*
younger brother (male speaking)	*taci-qu*
children	*luve-qu*

cousin

Note: if the cousin is the child of your father's brother or mother's sister, he/she is considered your brother or sister; otherwise:

cousin (male's male cousin)	*tavale-qu*
cousin (female's female cousin)	*dauve-qu, raiva-qu*
cousin (opposite-sex)	*tavale-qu, davola-qu*
daughter	*luve-qu (yalewa)*

daughter-in-law	*vugo-qu (yalewa)*
family	*iratou na weka-qu*
father	*tama-qu* or *no-qu tā*
father-in-law	*no-qu mōmō, vugo-qu*
grandfather	*tuka-qu*
grandmother	*bu-qu* or *no-qu būbū*
husband	*wati-qu*
husband and children	*no-qu veitamani*
mother	*tina-qu* or *no-qu nā*
mother-in-law	*no-qu nei, vugo-qu*
sister (male speaking)	*gāne-qu*
older sister (female speaking)	*tuaka-qu*
younger sister (female speaking)	*taci-qu*
son	*luve-qu (tagane)*
son-in-law	*vugo-qu (tagane)*
uncle (father's older brother)	*tama-qu levu* or *no-qu tā levu*
uncle (father's younger brother)	*tama-qu lailai* or *no-qu tā lailai*
uncle (mother's brother)	*no-qu mōmō, vugo-qu*
wife	*wati-qu*
wife and children	*no-qu veitinani*

Expressing Feelings

I am ...	*Au sā ...*
angry	*rarawa, cudru*
cold	*liliwa*
grateful	*vakavinavinaka*
happy	*mārau*
hot	*katakata*
hungry	*viakana*

in a hurry	*vakatotolo*
in trouble	*leqa*
right	*dina*
sad	*yalobībī, rarawa*
sleepy	*viamoce*
sorry (condolence)	*lomani iko/kemunī/koya etc*
thirsty	*viagunu*
tired	*oca, wawale*
well	*bula vinaka*
worried	*lomaleqa*
wrong	*cala*

Language Problems

I don't speak Fijian/English.	*Au sega ni kilā na vosa vakaviti/vakavālagi.*
I speak a little Fijian/English.	*Au kilā vakalailai na vosa vakaviti/vakavālagi.*
Do you speak English?	*O(nī) kilā na vosa vakavālagi?*
I understand.	*Sā macala.*
I don't understand.	*E sega ni macala.*
Could you repeat that?	*Tukuna tale mada.*
Could you speak more slowly please?	*Vosa mada vakamālua.*
Please show me (in this book).	*Vakaraitaka mada (ena ivola qō).*
I will look for it in this book.	*Au na vāqarā ena ivola qō.*
How do you say ... in Fijian?	*Cava na vakaviti ni ...?*
What does ... mean?	*Cava na ibalebale ni ...?*
What does this mean?	*Cava na kena ibalebale qō?*

Languages

Language names are formed simply by the noun *vosa*, 'language', and the prefix *vaka-* or *vā-* attached to the name of the country:

I speak ...	*Au kilā na vosa ...*
Danish	*vakadanimaki*
Dutch	*vakaōladi*
English	*vakavālagi*
French	*vakafaranisē*
German	*vakajāmani*
Japanese	*vakajāpani*
Norwegian	*vakanōwei*
Spanish	*vakasipeni*
Swedish	*vakasuiteni*

Interests

What do you do in your spare time?	*A cava o(nī) dau tāleitaka?*

I like ...	*Au tāleitaka na ...*
I don't like ...	*Au cata na ...*
Do you like ...?	*O(nī) tāleitaka na ...?*
dancing (Western)	*dānisi*
dancing (modern Fijian)	*tāralalā*
dancing (traditional Fijian)	*meke*
films	*sara iyaloyalo*
going shopping	*volivoli*
listening to music	*rogo sere*
playing cards	*veimau*
playing sports	*qito*
reading	*wilivola*

singing	*lagasere*
travelling	*gādē*
watching football	*sara veicaqe*
watching TV	*sara fīvī*
writing (corresponding)	*volavola*

Some Useful Phrases

What is this called?	*Cava na yacana qō?*
Can I take a photo?	*Au rawa ni veitaba?*
Sure.	*Rawa.*
Do you live here?	*O(nī) tiko i kē?*
Do you like it here?	*O(nī) tāleitaka i kē?*
Yes, a lot.	*Io, vakalevu.*
That's right.	*Donu.*
I don't know.	*Au sega ni kilā.*
Haven't a clue.	*Esi.*
That's true.	*Dina.*
That's a lie.	*Lasu.*
Me too.	*O yau tale gā.*
How are things?	*Vācava tiko?*
Fine.	*Totoka.*
Great.	*Wānanavu.*
So so.	*Vā gā yā.*

SMALL TALK

Getting Around

Fijians are always happy to help a stranger, so don't be shy about asking. At the same time, remember that part of Fiji's charm is its informality, and while there are such things as bus and ship timetables, they tend not to be taken very seriously, and people don't get very upset when things don't run according to schedule.

Finding Your Way

Where is the ...?
I vei na ...?

airport	*rārā ni waqavuka*
bus station (central)	*basten*
bus stop	*ikelekele ni basi*

What time does the ... leave/arrive?
Vica na kaloko e lako/kele kina na ...?

bus	*basi*
plane	*waqavuka*
boat	*waqa*

67

Directions

Where is ...?	*I vei na ...?*
How do I get to ...?	*I vei na sala i ...?*
Could you tell me where ... is?	*I vei beka o ...?*
Is it far?	*E yawa?*
Is it near here?	*E vōleka?*
Can I walk there?	*E rawa niu taubale kina?*
How far is it?	*E vāivei na kena yawa?*
Can you show me (on the map)?	*Vakaraitaka mada (ena mape).*
Are there other means of getting there?	*Eda lako tale kina vakacava?*
I want to go to the ... bus stop	*Au via lako i na ikelekele ni basi ni ...*
Go straight ahead.	*Vakadodonu.*
Next lamp-post.	*Dūrunicina qori.*
Turn left ...	*Gole i na imawī,* or *mawī ...*
Turn right ...	*Gole i na imatau,* or *matau ...*
Turn up (onto the street that goes up) ...	*Gole cake ...*
Turn down (onto the street that goes down) ...	*Gole sobu ...*
just here	*i kē gā*
further on	*i liu*
much further on	*i liu sara*
at the next corner	*mai na kona qori*
at the traffic lights	*mai na cina ni gaunisala*
You've gone past it!	*Sā sivi!*

behind	*daku-na*
far	*yawa*
in front of it	*mata-na*
near	*vōleka*
opposite	*veibāsai kei, dōnuya*

The most common reference points are trees and hedges:

by the ...	*i na ...*
coconut tree	*vuniniu*
mango tree	*vunimaqo*
breadfruit tree	*vuniuto*
rain tree	*vunivaivai*
hibiscus hedge	*bā senitoa*

Compass bearings (north etc) are never used. Instead one hears:

on the sea side of ...	*mai ... i wai*
on the land side of ...	*mai ... i vanua*
the far side of ...	*mai ... (yani) i liu*
this side of ...	*mai ... i muri*

Booking Tickets

It's unlikely you'll need Fijian in this situation, but you might have some fun trying it out.

I want to go to ...	*Au via lako i ...*
How much is it to go to ...	*E vica na ivodovodo i ...*
I'd like to book a seat to ...	*Au via sauma rawa dua na idabedabe i ...*
I would like a one-way ticket.	*Au via lako gā yani.*

I would like a return ticket.	*Au via lako lesu tale mai.*
Can I reserve a place?	*E rawa niu sauma rawa?*
Is it completely full?	*Sā sīnai sara gā?*
Please refund my ticket.	*Me vakasukai mada na noqu ilavo.*

Air

Even more unlikely you'll need Fijian here, but be prepared anyway!

Is there a flight to ...?	*E dua na waqavuka i ...?*
When is the next flight to ...?	*E dua tale na waqavuka i ... i na vica?*
How long does the flight take?	*Vica na dedē ni vuka?*

| customs | *kasitaba* |
| plane | *waqavuka* |

Bus

Local buses are one of the wonders of Fiji, very cheap and a lot of fun, except on a rainy day. Most local buses have no glass in the windows, but a rolled-up length of tarpaulin which you let down when it rains. There are designated bus stops, but in the country you can wave down a bus practically anywhere. In suburbs, bus stops are marked and generally adhered to where there is a bus shelter, but when there is no shelter people will wait under the nearest spreading mango or breadfruit tree. There is no queuing, and seldom any rush to get on. There are bus route numbers, but they are not generally known; people refer to buses by the places they go to *(basi ni Nasēsē, 'Nasēsē bus'; basi n valenibula,* 'hospital bus'; etc) and learn to recognise the different liveries (colour schemes).

Does this bus go to ...?	*Qō na basi i ...?*
Which bus goes to ...?	*I vei na basi i ...?*
Do the buses pass frequently?	*E dau levu na basi i kē?*
This is the hospital bus.	*Qō na basi ni vālenibula.*
This is the city bus.	*Qō na basi i na tāuni.*

You might try the next set of questions, but should be aware that bus timetables are generally closely guarded secrets, and often known to drivers only vaguely if at all. On the other hand, in most places in towns buses are frequent.

What time is the ...?	*Vica na kaloko na ...?*
next bus	*basi tarava*
first bus	*imatai ni basi*
last bus	*iotioti ni basi*

If you have bulky luggage, put it in the cargo space underneath the seats before you get on. You usually pay the driver when you get on. It is the custom in Fiji for men to give up their seats to women and the elderly. To stop the bus, you usually pull a cord running along either side. If you have an aisle seat, it is impolite to reach in front of the person beside you to pull the cord, so you attract their attention (eg. by tapping or scratching a couple of times on their thigh) and point to the cord. If you cannot get their attention in time, then reach for the cord saying *jilou.* There is no need to get up from your seat before the bus comes to a halt. If you have a window seat, say *au lako mada yani* to go past your fellow passenger, and likewise if there are standing passengers when you are getting off, saying *jilou* as you squeeze through. A couple of useful phrases:

Wait driver!	*Wāwā draiva!*
Could you let me know when we get to ...?	*Tukuna mada vei au meu sobu mai ...*
I want to get off!	*Au sobu!*
Excuse me. (reaching to pull the cord)	*Jilou.*
Excuse me. (to get past people)	*Au lako mada yani.*
Thanks driver!	*Vinaka draiva!*

Taxi

Taxis can be hired from stands or flagged down on the street with the arm outstretched and the hand beckoning palm downwards. If the driver does not see you flagging, a sudden loud hiss will do the trick. Most taxis are metred now, especially in towns, but if not the fare should be agreed on beforehand. Men usually sit in front with the driver. There is no tipping. The following phrases are primarily intended for use with Fijian taxi drivers (who are in the minority), but quite a few Indian taxi drivers also speak a rough and ready Fijian.

Can you take me to ...?	*Au via lako i ...*
How much does it cost to go to ...?	*Vica na ivodovodo i ...?*
It's too much!	*Sā sīvia!*
How much do I owe you?	*Vica beka yā?*
I want a taxi to the airport.	*Me dua na teksi i rārā ni waqavuka.*
Blow your horn please.	*Tagi mada na sici.*

Instructions

Here is fine, thank you.	*Rauta i kē, vinaka.*
The next corner, please.	*Gole i liu qori.*
Continue!	*Lako!*
The next street to the left.	*Gaunisala qori ina imawī.*
Stop here!	*Kele!*
Please slow down.	*Vakamālua mada.*
Please hurry.	*Vakatotolo mada.*
Please wait (here).	*Wāwā mada (i kē).*

Hitching

The thumbs-up sign is hardly known in Fiji; if you need a lift, you wave down a car and they usually stop. The practice of hitching is not popular but sometimes it's the only way to get to places, short of walking.

I'm going to ...	*A lako i ...*
Are you going to ...?	*O(nī) lako i ...?*
Are you passing ...?	*O(nī) na volekati ...?*
Thanks for the ride.	*Vinaka vakalevu na veikau.*

Car

Road signs and driving courtesies are much the same as in Australia and New Zealand, if observed with a little less rigour. Even on the main highway, one must always be prepared for the unexpected, such as wandering livestock and young men pounding kava on the road. Two customs in particular will be unfamiliar to some. Those from outside Australasia should note that the signal to a following driver that the road ahead is clear to overtake is to activate the *right* indicator. This means of course that if you are following a vehicle and the right indicator flashes, it may mean either 'please overtake, the road ahead is clear' or 'I am about to turn right, so if you attempt to overtake me there will be a collision'. Best to stay put.

Another is that all traffic stops as a sign of respect when a funeral cortege comes from the opposite direction. The lead car of the procession usually has its headlights on, so there may be some warning, but often the first thing you know is when the car ahead of you comes to a sudden halt for no apparent reason.

Where can I rent a car?	*I vei e tū kina na motokā saumi?*
Where's the next petrol station?	*I vei tale e dua na itawatawa ni benisini?*
Please fill the tank.	*Me vakasīnai mada.*
I want ... litres of petrol (gas).	*Me ... na lita na benisini.*
Ten dollars worth please.	*Kerea mada e tini na dola.*
Please check the oil and water.	*Raica mada na waiwai kei na wai.*
Please wash the windscreen.	*Qusi mada na iloilo.*
How long can I park here?	*Au rawa ni kele i kē vica na aua?*
Does this road lead to?	*Qō na gaunisala i ...?*

Problems

The battery is flat.	*Sā maca na betirī.*
The radiator is leaking.	*Sā turu na reidieita.*
I have a flat tyre.	*Au sā panja.*
It's overheating.	*Sā katakata na idini.*
It's not working.	*Sā mate tū.*

Useful Words

accelerator	*sipiti*
battery	*betirī*
brakes	*bereki*
clutch	*kalaji*
driver's licence	*laiseni (ni draiva)*
engine	*idini*
give way	*wāwā*
horn	*sici*
lights	*cina*
mechanic	*mekeniki*
oil	*waiwai*
puncture	*panja*
radiator	*reidieita*
road map	*mape (ni gaunisala)*
stop	*kele*
tyres	*taya*
windscreen	*iloilo (i liu)*

Boat

Some of the outer islands are accessible by plane, but boats are still a popular means of inter-island transport. The more expensive class is 'saloon'; if you wish to mingle with the hoi polloi, travel by 'deck'. Eating arrangements vary from boat to boat, so check beforehand.

boat	*waqa*
dock	*wavu*
life-jacket	*iqaloqalo*

Some Useful Phrases

What about eating on board?	*Vakacava na kana i waqa?*
Bring your own.	*Dui kau kena.*
Meals are served.	*E vakarautaki na kākana.*
There's a 'canteen' (small shop which sells basic foods).	*E tiko na kentin.*
The boat is delayed/cancelled/on time.	*Sā toso/daro/donu na lako ni waqa.*
How long will it be delayed?	*Ena qai lako ina vica?* (lit 'what time will it go?')
How long does the trip take?	*Vica na dedē ni soko?*
Is it a direct route?	*E muri vakadodonu?*
Is that seat taken?	*E dua e dabe i keri?*
I want to get off at ...	*Au via sobu i ...*
Excuse me (when wishing to go past someone).	*Au lako mada yani.*
Where is the rest room?	*I vei na valelailai?*
I feel seasick.	*Au via lua.*

Some Useful Words

above	*i cake*
address	*edres, itikotiko*
around here	*vanua qō*
arrival	*yaco*
below	*i rā*
bicycle	*basikeli*
bus stop	*ikelekele ni basi*
cancel	*daro*
confirm	*vakadeitaka*
Danger! Careful!	*Qarauna!*
departure	*lako, biubiu*
deposit	*ivakadei*
early	*totolo*
map	*mape*
non-smoking	*tabu na vakatavako*
one-way (ticket)	*lako yani*
over there	*mai keā*
return (ticket)	*lako yani lesu mai*
seat	*idabedabe*
smoking	*vakatavako*
Stop!	*Kele!*
ticket	*tikite*
to the side	*i yasana*
Wait!	*Wāwā!*

Accommodation

There is a variety of accomodation in Fiji, all geared primarily to the English-speaking tourist. As always, however, Fijians will appreciate your attempts to speak the local language.

Accommodation available ranges from backpacker dorms to five-star hotels. Such is the hospitality of Fijians, that even a chance acquaintance may lead to your being invited to stay with a Fijian family. If this happens, prepare yourself by reading the last section in this chapter (page 84).

Where is ...?   *I vei ...*
  a guesthouse   *dua na bure ni vulagi*
  a hotel   *dua na ōtela*

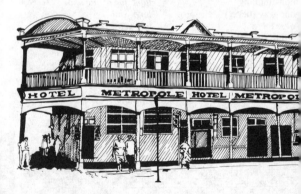

A note of caution. The term 'guesthouse' and its Fijian equivalent often refer to establishments offering rooms for hire by the hour for the purpose of clandestine liaisons.

What street?	*Gaunisala cava?*

I am looking for ... *Au vāqarā ...*
   a cheap hotel   *e dua na ōtela sau māmada*
   a clean hotel   *e dua na ōtela savasavā*
   a good hotel   *e dua na ōtela vinaka*
   a nearby hotel   *e dua na ōtela vōleka*

Could you write down the address please? *Volā mada na edres.*

At the Hotel
Checking In

Do you have any rooms available? *Bau dua na rumu?*

I would like ... *Au vinakata ...*
   a single room   *na rumu taudua*
   a double room   *na rumu taurua*
   a room with a private   *na rumu vakavalenisili*
     bathroom
   to share a dorm   *meu moce gā i bure*
   a bed   *e dua na imocemoce*

I want a room with a ... *Au vinakata na rumu*
   bathroom   *vakavalenisili*
   shower   *vakasawa*

TV	*vakatīvī*
window	*vākātubaleka*

How much is it per night?	*Yāvica dua na bogi?*
Can I see the room?	*Au raica mada na rumu.*
Are there any others?	*Tiko tale e dua?*
Are there any cheaper rooms?	*Tiko tale e dua e sau lailai?*
Is there a discount for students?	*E lutusobu vei ira na gonevuli?*
Do you allow children?	*Era vakatarai na gone?*
Is there a discount for children?	*E lutusobu vei ira na gone?*
Does it include breakfast?	*E wili kina na ikatalau?*
It's fine, I'll take it.	*Daumaka, au sa na taura.*

Some Useful Phrases

I'm going to stay for ...	*Au na ...*
one day	*siga dua*
two days	*siga rua*
one week	*mācawa dua*

I'm not sure how long I'm staying.	*Sega ni macala na dedē ni noqu tiko.*
Is there a lift?	*E dua na liva?*
Where is the bathroom (for washing)?	*I vei na valenisili?*
Where is the bathroom (toilet)?	*I vei na valelailai?*
Is there hot water all day?	*E lako tū gā na wai katakata?*
Could you store this/these for me?	*Māroroi mada qō.*

Do you have a safe where I can leave my valuables?	*E dua na sefi me māroroi kina noqu iyau drēdrē?*
Do I leave my key at reception?	*Me dau biu na kī ina 'reception'?*
Is there somewhere to wash clothes?	*E dua na vanua ni savasava?*
Can I use the kitchen?	*Au rawa ni vakayagataka na valenikuro?*
Could I use the telephone?	*Au kerea mada na talevoni.*
Could someone look after my child?	*E rawa ni dua e raica noqu gone?*
Please wake me up at … tomorrow.	*Meu vakayadrati mada ina … nimataka.*
The room needs to be cleaned.	*Na rumu me sāmaki.*
Please change the sheets.	*Veisau mada na itutuvi.*
I'd like to pay now.	*Au sā sauma mada qō.*

Requests & Complaints

Excuse me, something's the matter.	*I kemunī, e dua tiko na leqa.*
I have a request.	*E dua noqu kerekere.*
The door/window is jammed.	*E tāō tū na kātuba/kātubaleka.*
I can't close the door/window.	*E sega ni sogo rawa na kātuba/kātubaleka.*
I've locked myself out of my room.	*Au sā sogoti au i tuba.*
The toilet won't flush.	*E sega ni lako na wai ni valelailai.*
The … doesn't work.	*E cā tū na …*

Can you get it fixed?	*E rawa ni vakavinakataki?*
I've lost the key.	*Au sā vakayalia na kī.*
I don't like this room.	*E cā vei au na rumu qō.*
It's too small.	*E lailai.*
It's too cold/hot.	*E batabatā/katakata.*
It's noisy.	*E kosakosā.*
It's too dark.	*E butō.*
It's expensive.	*E saulevu.*
It smells.	*E boi.*
It's dirty.	*E duka.*

Checking Out

I would like to check out ...	*Au via vāgalala ...*
now	*qō*
at noon	*ina sigalevu*
tomorrow	*nimataka*
I would like to pay the bill.	*Au via sauma na bili.*
Can I leave my luggage here?	*Biu mada i kē noqu iyāyā.*
I'm returning ...	*Au na lesu mai ...*
tomorrow	*nimataka*
in a few days	*ni oti e siga vica*

Some Useful Words

address	*edres*
air-conditioned	*vakabatabatātaki*
babysitter	*meimei*
balcony	*varada*

bathroom	*valenisili*
bed	*imocemoce*
bill	*bili*
blanket	*vulāqeti*
candle	*kādrala*
chair	*idabedabe*
clean	*savasavā*
cold	*batabatā*
cupboard	*kōvate*
dark	*butō*
dirty	*duka*
double bed	*imocemoce taurua*
electricity	*livaliva*
excluded	*sega ni wili*
electric fan	*irinicagi*
hot	*katakata*
included	*wili kina*
key	*kī*
lift (elevator)	*liva*
light bulb	*matanicina, 'globe'*
lock (n)	*loka*
mattress	*meteresi*
mirror	*iloilo*
padlock	*loka, iviqāqā*
pillow	*ilokoloko*
quiet	*vakadīrorogo*
room	*rumu*
sheet	*siti, itutuvi*
shower	*sawa*
soap	*sovu*
suitcase	*kato(nisulu)*

table	*tēveli*
toilet	*valelailai*
toilet paper	*pepa ni valelailai*
towel	*tauelu*
water	*wai*
cold water	*wai liliwa*
hot water	*wai katakata*
window	*kātubaleka*

Staying with a Family

Should you be invited to stay with a Fijian family, prepare yourself for a novel and heartwarming experience. Fijians are masters at entertaining, and go out of their way to make guests feel as comfortable as possible. You will probably be given the best room in the house (or, if in a village, the only bed), and served with the best foods, within your host's means.

When you arrive, bring with you some *yaqona* (kava). This is for your *sevusevu* – a formal presentation, comparable to bringing a bottle of wine when you visit. In towns it's acceptable to bring a few bags of pounded yaqona *(taga yaqona)*, which is available in small shops, some markets, service stations and many private houses. For a more classy entrance, buy a bundle of *waka* (kava roots), available at markets and some shops and service stations.

Some phrases you may need are:

Where can I buy yaqona?	*E volitaki i vei na yaqona?*
What kind of yaqona?	*Yaqona cava?*
ground yaqona (inferior but cheap)	*yaqona qaqi*
pounded yaqona	*yaqona tuki*
a bundle of yaqona root	*dua na ivesu waka*

Mary sells it from her house.	*E dau bāeti o Mere.*
How much for one bag?	*E vica dua na taga?*

Soon after arriving at the house, tell your host that you would like to *sevusevu*:

I've bought a little yaqona.	*Dua na yaqona lailai au kanta mai.*

You will not, of course, be expected to actually present it yourself. In a village, your host may accept it himself, or take you to the *valelevu* (chief's house) for it to be presented to the local *tūraga* (chief).

When you are about to leave, you should present another yaqona as your *itatau* (farewell offering).

For behaviour inside a Fijian home, see sections on eating and drinking yaqona in the Greetings & Civilities chapter (pages 54 to 55). If you need anything, don't be afraid to ask:

Could I have ...?	*Au kere ...?*
a towel	*tauelu*
toilet paper	*pepa ni valelailai*
soap	*sovu*
salt	*māsima*
a wraparound cloth	*isulu vakatoga*

If in a village, you may be an object of curiosity, and many people will want to shake your hand and ask you questions about yourself. If you're there on a Sunday, you will be required to attend the morning church service, and may be formally welcomed.

A note of warning: please try to be sensitive. The dictates of Fijian hospitality require that you be looked after as long as you stay. Nobody will tell you to leave nor will anybody ask you to contribute to the household. But to be fair, you should make a regular contribution, in cash or, preferably, store goods. Hand them quietly to the woman of the house, saying something like *Dua noqu kā ni veivuke lailai* (Just a little help from me). When about to leave, give some small presents for them to remember you by. If you would like to give cash, you might say it's for the kids' school fees *(icurucuru ni vuli)* or to buy sugar with *(ivoli ni suka)*. Your gift will be accepted with a short expression of thanks and clapping *(cobo)*.

Around Town

Towns are where English reigns supreme, but you can create a little warmth and perhaps a little mirth by trying out your Fijian on unsuspecting locals.

I'm looking for ...	*Au vāqarā ...*
a bank	*na baqe*
a church	*na valenilotu*
the city centre	*na loma ni tāuni*
the ... embassy	*na ebasī/valenivolavola ni ...*
my hotel	*noqu ōtela*
the market	*na mākete*
the museum	*na vale ni yau māroroi*
the police	*na ovisa*
the post office	*na posi(tōvesi)*
a public toilet	*na valelailai*
a restaurant	*e dua na valenikana*
the tourist information office	*na valenivolavola ni saravanua*

What time does it open?	*E dola ina vica?*
What time does it close?	*E sogo ina vica?*

What ... is this?	*Na ... cava qō?*
street	*gaunisala*
street number	*naba ni vale*
suburb	*vanua*

87

Note: For directions, see the Getting Around chapter (pg 68).

At the Post Office

I would like to send ...	*Au via vākau ...*
a letter	*ivola*
a parcel	*ioloolo*
a telegram	*telekaramu*

I would like some stamps.	*Au via voli sitaba.*
How much is the postage?	*Vica na isau ni sitaba?*
How much is it to send this to ...?	*Vica na isau ni kena vākau i ...?*

Some Useful Words

envelope	*waqanivola*
mail box	*katonimeli*
parcel	*ioloolo*
stamp	*sitaba*

Telephone

All telephone operators speak English, in fact some get annoyed if you speak Fijian to them (they consider it professionally demeaning). The following might however be useful in the more rural areas, where the operator is more likely to appreciate your efforts.

I want to call ...	*Au via qiri i ...*
The number is ...	*Na naba na ...*
How much does a three-minute call cost?	*Vica na kena isau me tolu na miniti?*

I'll call you back.	*Au na qiri tale yani.*
How much does each extra minute cost?	*Vica me dua tale na miniti?*
I want to make a reverse-charges phone call.	*Au via qiri me saumi mai yasana dua.*
I would like to speak to ...	*Au vosa mada vei ...*
Hello, do you speak English?	*Bula, nī kilā na vosa vakavālagi?*
Hello, is ... there?	*Bula, e tiko qori o ...?*
Yes, he/she is here.	*Io, e tiko qō.*
One moment, please.	*Wāwā mada.*
It's engaged.	*E oso.*
Operator, I've been cut off.	*Opereita, sā mate tale.*

At the Bank

Banks are another bastion of English, but you could bring a little brightness into the dreariest of days with the following.

I want to exchange some money.	*Au via veisau ilavo.*
How many Fiji dollars per dollar?	*Vica na dola ni Viti dua na dola?*
Can I have money transferred here from my bank?	*E rawa niu vākau ilavo mai noqu baqe i kē?*
How long will it take to arrive?	*E na vica na kena dedē qai yaco mai?*
I'm expecting some money from ...	*Au wāraka e dua na ilavo mai ...*
Has my money arrived yet?	*Sā yaco mai na noqu ilavo?*
Sign here.	*Saini i kē.*

Sightseeing

Where is the tourist office?	*I vei na valenivolavola ni saravanua?*
What's ...?	*Cava ... ?*
this/that building	*na vale qō/yā*
this/that monument	*na ivakananumi qō/yā*
What time does it open/close?	*E dola/sogo ina vica?*
Do you have a map?	*E dua nomu(nī) mape?*

Fijians generally appreciate having their photographs taken, especially with visitors, but it is best to ask first.

Can I take photographs?	*E rawa na veitaba?*
Can I take your photograph?	*Au tabaki iko/kemudrau/ kemudou/kemunī mada.*
I'll send you the photograph.	*Au na vākauta yani na itaba.*
Could you take a photograph of me?	*Tabaki au mada.*

Some Useful Words

(swimming) beach	*bāravi nuku*
building	*vale*
church	*valenilotu*
market	*mākete*
monument	*ivakananumi*

statue	*ivakatākarakara*
university	*univesitī*

AROUND TOWN

Night Life

What is there to do in the evenings?	*Cava e bau dau caka ina bogi?*
Are there any night clubs?	*E tiko na valenidānisi?*
Are there places where you can hear local music?	*E tiko na vanua ni rogo sere vakaviti?*
How much does it cost to get in?	*Vīca na icurucuru?*

I would like to watch ...	*Au via sara ...*
boxing	*veivacu*
rugby	*rakavī*
soccer	*soka*
cricket	*kirikiti*

Some Useful Words

bar	*valenigunu*
cinema	*valeniyaloyalo*
kava bar	*valeniyaqona*
nightclub/discotheque	*valenidānisi*

In the Country

It is important to realise that in Fiji nowhere is nobody's. Even the most desolate-looking areas and the densest forest have owners who have a profound, almost mystical, attachment to their land. By all means explore, picnic, swim in the river and so on, but leave the place as you found it. To camp, you should seek permission, and present an *isevusevu* and *itatau* (see the Accommodation chapter, pages 84 to 85). Places with a high concentration of cultivated plants (coconuts, mangoes, etc) are probably old villages, and should be avoided; likewise places with stands of red-leaved plants such as crotons and cordyline, which are probably burial grounds. Many caves are also old burial places.

If you would like to see round a village, don't just walk straight in. Talk to someone and say: *Au sarasara mada e loma ni koro* (I'd like to look round the village) and they'll be happy to show you round.

Weather

What's the weather like?	*Vakacava tiko na draki?*
The weather is ... today.	*E ... nikua.*
Will it be ... tomorrow?	*E na ... nimataka?*
cold	*batabatā*
cloudy	*rugurugua*
humid	*tunumaka/vākatakata*
hot	*katakata*
very hot!	*katakata sara!*
raining	*tau na uca*
windy	*bula na cagi*

92

Some Useful Words

cloud	*ō*
dry season	*vulaisiga*
earth	*vuravura*
hurricane	*cagilaba*
lightning	*livaliva*
mist	*kabu*
mud	*sōsō*
rain	*uca*
the rainy season	*vulaiuca*
storm	*draki cā*
sun	*siga*
thunder	*kurukuru*
weather	*draki*
wind	*cagi*

IN THE COUNTRY

Seasons

spring	*vulaitubutubu*
summer	*vulaikatakata*
autumn	*vulaimatumatua*
winter	*vulaililiwa*
rainy season	*vulaiuca*
dry season	*vulaisiga*

Some Useful Words

agriculture	*teitei*
bay	*toba*
beach (landing)	*matāsawa*
bridge	*wavu*
cave	*qaravatu*
city	*siti*

country person	*tū vakavanua*
earthquake	*uneune*
farm	*iteitei*
forest	*veikau*
grassland	*veicō*, (reed-covered) *talāsiga*
harbour	*ikelekele ni waqa*
headland	*ucuna*
hill	*delana*
hot spring	*waikatakata*
island	*yanuyanu*
jungle	*veikauloa*
lake	*drano*
landslide	*sisi na qele*
mountain	*ulunivanua*
mountain range	*veidelana*
ocean	*wasawasa*
pool (for swimming)	*tobunisili*
reef	*cakau*
river	*uciwai*
village	*koro*
waterfall	*savu*

Animals, Sea Creatures, etc

bat	*beca*
cat	*pusi*
coral	*lase*
cow	*bulumakau*
crab	*qari*
dog	*kolī*
domestic animal	*manumanu susu*
fish	*ika*

frog	boto ni Viti
goat	mē
horse	ose
iguana	vōkai
land crab	lairo
lizard	moko
lobster	urau
mangrove lobster	manā
mongoose	manipusi
octopus	kuita
pig	vuaka
rat	kalavo
sheep	sipi
snake	gata
toad	boto
turtle	vonu
bush animal/bird	manumanu ni veikau

IN THE COUNTRY

Birds

bird	manumanuvuka
chicken	toa
duck	gā
heron	belō
mynah	mainā
parrot	kakā
owl	lulu
pigeon (bush)	soqe
pigeon (town)	ruve
rooster	tamanitoa
seagull	drē, icō

Insects

ant	*qasikālōlō*
butterfly	*bēbē*
centipede	*cikinovu*
cockroach	*kokoroti*
fly	*lago*
lice	*kutu*
mosquito	*namu*
spider	*viritālawalawa*

Plants

bamboo	*bitu*
coconut	*niu*
firewood	*buka*
flower	*sē(nikau)*
hibiscus	*senitoa*
leaf	*drau(nikau)*

mango	*maqo*
mangrove	*dogo*
pawpaw	*weleti*
sugar cane	*dovu*
tree	*vu(nikau)*
wood	*kau*

Camping

Camping is very rare in Fiji. The natural reaction of a Fijian to a camper is to feel great pity and insist on bringing them home to a decent house. It's prohibited to camp on village land without permission. However, if you insist:

Am I allowed to camp here?	*E rawa ni biri i kē noqu valelaca?*

backpack	*idrekedreke*
can opener	*idolanitini*
compass	*kābasi*
firewood	*buka*
mattress	*meteresi*
penknife	*iseleloki*
rope	*dali*
tent	*valelaca*
torch (flashlight)	*cina livaliva*
stove	*parāmasi*
water bottle	*tavaya ni wai*

Some Useful Phrases

Can one swim here?	*E rawa na sīsili i kē?*
What's that animal called?	*Cava na yaca ni manumanu yā?*
What's that plant called?	*Cava na yaca ni kau yā?*
What's this fish called?	*Cava na yaca na ika qō?*
Can I get there on foot/on horseback?	*E rawa niu taubale/vodoose kina?*
Do I need a guide?	*Me dua me kauti au?*
Can someone take me there?	*Erawa ni dua e kauti au kina?*
How much might that cost?	*E na vica beka na kana isau?*

You'll find that, unless they are very used to tourists, Fijians will feel uncomfortable with this last question. Even if they say nothing, you should pay them something if you are asking them to be guides.

Food

All kinds of food are available in shops and supermarkets, but local produce is sold in markets and roadside stalls, always good places to improve your Fijian. For eateries, Fijian is more likely to be spoken at the lower end of the range, in some of the Chinese restaurants and in stalls where town Fijians and market vendors get large helpings of Fijian food for very little cost. If you are accustomed to local food and eating conditions, these stalls are very good value.

restaurant	*valenikana*
cheap restaurant	*valenikana saurawarawa*
Chinese restaurant	*valenikana ni kai Jaina*
Indian restaurant	*valenikana ni kai Idia*
food vendor	*volitaki kākana*
breakfast	*katalau*
lunch	*vakasigalevu*
dinner	*vakayakavi*
to eat	*kana*, (tr) *kania*
to drink	*gunu-va*

Special Dishes

Fijians are fond of a wide variety of dishes, including European, Chinese, and Indian. Curries are especially popular, as is chop-suey, even in Fijian villages.

goat curry	*kari mē*
chicken curry	*kari toa*
fish curry	*suruwā*

A typical Fijian meal consists of two components: a boiled (or earth-oven baked) root vegetable, and what is called the *icoi*, fish or meat and/or a green vegetable. The root vegetable is often one of the following:

breadfruit	*uto*
cassava	*tavioka*
cooking banana	*vudi*
sweet potato	*kumala*
taro	*dalo*
wild yam	*utikau, rauva, tīvoli*
yam	*uvi*

There are many Fijian greens, the most popular being:

bele	'island cabbage' is one English name, but in Fiji it's always known by its Fijian name
duruka	called 'Fiji asparagus' but actually related to sugar-cane
lumi	seaweed
moca or *tubua*	a kind of spinach
ota	fern leaves
rourou	taro leaves

FOOD

Methods of Cooking

When something is cooked in coconut cream it is said to be *vakalolo* (not to be confused with the same words, *vakalolo*, meaning a kind of sweet pudding); when baked in the earth-oven it is said to be *vavi*; fried is *tavuteke*; when served with fermented coconut, *kora*, it is said to be *vākora*.

Apart from salt and occasionally chillies, condiments are rarely used.

Local Dishes

The following is a small selection of local *icoi* you are likely to encounter and may be unfamiliar with.

ika vakalolo
Fish boiled in coconut cream, often with a green vegetable. Note that the fish is served whole and the head is the most highly esteemed part.

kokoda
Marinated raw fish or shellfish (actually more popular among tourists than Fijians)

kuita vakalolo
Octopus stewed in coconut cream.

lairo vakasoso
Landcrab, *lairo*, meat stuffed in the shell with coconut cream, chopped onions etc.

palusami
Corned beef and coconut cream wrapped in *rourou* (taro leaves) and baked in the earth-oven.

vuaka vavi
Pork baked whole in the earth-oven.

The following are some Fijian desserts and snacks (eaten at any time):

ivi
Boiled Tahitian chestnuts, usually sold wrapped in a kind of taro-leaf parcel.

ōtai
'Fijian fruit salad', unripe mango grated, sweetened with sugar, and served with grated coconut.

vakalolo
'Fijian pudding' of many kinds, essentially baked and pounded vegetable root served in a syrup or with grated coconut.

vudi vakasoso
Ripe cooking banana served in thick coconut cream with grated coconut.

Roadside and market vendors also sell all kinds of fresh fruit (see further below) and snacks such as *silā* (boiled maize/corn), *dovu* (sugar cane), *pinati* (peanuts) and *bini* (spiced peas, originally an Indian food).

FOOD

At the Restaurant

Table for ... please.	*Keitou lē ...*
Waiter!/Waitress!	*I kemunī!*
Can I see the menu please?	*Au raica mada na ivolanik-ana/meniu.*
What is the soup of the day?	*Supu cava nikua?*
What is this/that?	*Cava qō/yā?*
I would like ...	*Au kerea na ...*
Another ..., please.	*Dua tale mada na ...*
Nothing more?	*Sā kua?*

Anything else? — *Dua tale na kā?*
I am hungry. — *Au viakana.*
I am thirsty. — *Au viagunu.*

The meal was delicious. — *Maleka sara na kākana.*
Do you have sauce? — *Tiko na sos?*
Not too spicy please. — *Me kua soti mada ni gaga.*
It's not hot. — *E sega ni gaga.*
Please bring me ... — *Au kerea mada ...*

Vegetarian

I am a vegetarian. — *Au tabu lēwenimanumanu.*
I don't eat beef/pork — *Au tabu bulumakau/vuaka.*
I don't eat dairy products. — *Au tabu sucu kei na jisi.*
(literally 'milk and cheese')

Meat

beef — *bulumakau*
chicken — *toa*
duck — *gā*
fat — *uro*
goat — *mē*
ham — *'ham', saganivuaka*

FOOD

heart	*uto*
lamb	*lami*
liver	*yate*
meat	*lewe(nimanumanu)*
mutton	*māteni*
pork	*vuaka*
roast beef/pork	*bulumakau/vuaka vavi*
sausage	*sōseti*
medium	*buta donu*
rare	*buta droka*
well done	*buta matua*

Seafood

clams	*kaikoso*
crab	*qari*
eel	*duna*
fish	*ika*

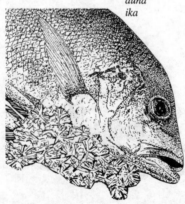

lobster	*urau*
mussels	*kuku*
oyster	*dio*
prawns	*ura*
shark	*qiō*
shellfish	*vivili*
shrimps	*moci*
squid	*kuita*
tuna	*yatu/tuna*

Vegetables

beans	*bini*
cabbage	*kāveti*
carrot	*kāreti*
corn	*silā*
cucumber	*kiukaba*
eggplant	*baigani*
lettuce	*lētisi*
mushrooms	*daliganikau*
onion	*varasa*
potato	*pateta*
pumpkin	*vavukeni*
spinach (local)	*tubua/moca*
sweet potato	*kumala*
tomato	*tōmata*
vegetable (green)	*draunikau*

Fruit

fruit	*vua(nikau)*
apple	*yāpolo*
avocado	*pea*

FOOD

banana	*jaina*
chestnut (local, sometimes called 'Tahitian chestnut')	*ivi*
coconut	*niu,* (for drinking) *bū*
guava	*quawa*
lemon	*molikaro*
Malay apple	*kavika*
mandarin	*maderini*
nut (Barringtonia)	*vutu*
orange	*moli taiti*
papaya	*weleti*
passionfruit	*qaranidila*
pineapple	*vaināviu*
Polynesian plum, Oceanic lychee	*dawa*
Tahitian apple	*wī*
watermelon	*mēleni*

Dairy Products

butter	*bata*
cheese	*jisi*
cream	*kirimu*
ice cream	*aiskrim*
margarine	*majerini*
milk	*sucu*

Eggs

boiled eggs	*yaloka saqa*
egg	*yaloka*
fried eggs	*yaloka tavuteke*
scrambled eggs	*yaloka qaqi*

Breads & Cereals

bread	*madrai*
buns	*bani*
cake	*keke*
corn	*silā*
flour	*falawa*
pancake	*panikeke (waicala)*
porridge	*pōreti*
rice	*raisi*
savoury biscuits	*bisikete*
scones	*sikoni*
sweet	*kamikamica*
sweet biscuits	*keke*
toast	*tosi/madrai tavu*

FOOD

Condiments

chilli	*rōkete/boro*
cinnamon	*sināmoni*
garlic	*qāliki*
ginger	*didiā*
lemon juice	*wai ni molikaro*
oil	*waiwai*
onion	*varasa*
pepper	*pepa*
salt	*māsima*
soy sauce	*soi*
sugar	*suka*
vinegar	*vinika*

Miscellaneous Food

dessert	*ivakalomavinaka, ivakalau*
honey	*denioni*
jam	*jamu*
sandwich	*seniwiji*
soup	*supu*

Cooking Methods

baked	*vavi*
barbecued	*tavu/babakiu*
boiled	*saqa*
fried	*tavuteke*
grilled	*tavu*
in coconut milk	*vakalolo*
roasted	*vavi*
steamed	*buta ina cawā*
stir-fried	*qisi*

FOOD

Drinks

beer	*bia*
cold drink	*wai batabatā*
ice	*aisi*
juice	*wai(nimoli)*
orange juice	*wainimoli*
spirits	*yaqona ni vālagi*
water	*wai*
wine	*waini*
without ice	*kua na aisi*

Hot Drinks

black coffee	*kofi loaloa*
a coffee	*kofi*
with milk	*vakasucu*
without milk	*kua na sucu*
without sugar	*kua na suka*
cocoa, hot chocolate	*koko*
lemon leaves	*draunimoli*
lemon-grass tea	*cōboi*
tea	*tī*

Some Useful Words

ashtray	*eshtrei*
baby food	*kedra na gone*
the bill	*na bili*
bowl	*boulu*
cold	*batabatā*
cup	*bilo*
a fork	*icula*
fresh	*bulabula*

FOOD

glass	*bilo iloilo*
a knife	*isele*
napkin	*iqūsiniliga*
a plate	*veleti*
ripe	*dreu*
spicy	*gaga*
a spoon	*itaki*
stale	*bulagi*
sweet	*kamikamica*
teaspoon	*itaki ni fī*
toothpick	*ileu ni bati*

FOOD

Shopping

Perhaps the most important expression to have prepared when you go shopping is *sarasara gā*, ('I'm just looking'), which will keep the assistant off your back at least temporarily, and might even get you taken for a local.

I would like to buy ...	*Au kerea mada ...*
How much is it?	*E vica?*
Do you have others?	*Tiko tale e sō?*
I don't like it.	*E cā vei au.* (or just grunt and shake your head)
Can I see it?	*Au raica mada?*
I'll take (buy) it.	*Au sā volia.*
There is none/We don't have any.	*E sega (vei keitou).*
Which one?	*Koya i vei?*
This one?	*Koya qō?*
Show it to me.	*Vakaraitaka.*
Can I look at it?	*Au raica mada?*
Do you accept credit cards?	*Au rawa ni sauma ina 'credit card'?*
What is it made of?	*E buli mai na cava?*
What material is it?	*Na isulu cava?*
Where can I buy ...?	*E volitaki i vei na ...?*
Where is the nearest ...?	*I vei e dua na ... vōleka i kē?*
bookshop	*sitoa ni vola*
clothing store	*sitoa ni sulu*

111

laundry	*valenisavasava*
market	*mākete*
pharmacy	*kēmesi*
shop	*sitoa*
shoeshop	*sitoa ni vāvā*
souvenir shop	*sitoa ni saravanua*
supermarket	*supamākete*
vegetable shop	*sitoa ni kākana*

Bargaining

Bargaining is the norm in duty-free shops and in some souvenir markets and stalls, but not in other shops or in the food markets.

That's very expensive!	*Sā sau levu!*
That's too expensive for me.	*Au sega ni rawata.*
Really?	*Dina?*
The price is very high.	*Sā sīvia na kena isau.*
I don't have much money.	*E lailai noqu ilavo.*
Could you lower the price?	*E rawa ni lutu na kena isau?*
I'll give you ...	*Au rawa ni solia ...*
No more than ...	*Kua ni sīvia na ...*

Souvenirs

| bark cloth | *masi* |
| club | *iwau* |

earrings	*sau*
garland	*salusalu*
grass skirt	*liku (vau)*
handicraft	*cakacaka ni liga*
kava bowl	*tānoa*
mask	*matavulo*
mats	*ibe*
necklace	*itaube*

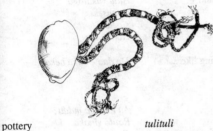

pottery	*tulituli*
ring	*mama*
shells	*gānivivili*
wood carvings	*sivisivi*

Clothing

bra	*ivakamoko*
clothing	*isulu*
coat	*kote*
dress	*vinivō*
hat	*isala*
jacket	*jākete*
jeans	*lī*

jumper, pullover	*siqileti ni katakata*
pocket sulu	*isulu vakataga*
sandals	*ivāvā ni ovisa*
shirt	*sote*
shoes	*ivāvā*
shorts	*tarausese lekaleka*
skirt	*liku*
socks	*stōkini*
sulu (wraparound)	*isulu vakatoga*
trousers	*tarausese*
T shirt	*siqeleti*
underwear	*isuluiloma*

I want something like ...	*Me dua e vakā beka ...*
this/these	*qō*
that/those	*yā*

Can I try it on?	*Au tovolea mada?*
It fits well.	*Rauta vinaka.*
It doesn't fit (too tight).	*E oso.*
It doesn't fit (too large).	*E galala.*

It is too ...	*E ...*
big	*levu*
small	*lailai*
short	*lekaleka*
long	*balavu*
tight	*oso*
loose	*galala*

Can it be altered?	*E rawa ni cula tale?*

Materials

cotton	*isulu dina*
handmade	*culaliga*
leather	*leca*
nylon	*nailoni*
silk	*silika*
wool	*kula*

Colours

black	*loaloa*
blue	*karakarawa*
brown	*braun, masikuvui*
dark	*butō*
green	*drokadroka*
light	*rārama*
orange	*seninawanawa*
pink	*piqi*
purple	*lokaloka*
red	*damudamu*
white	*vulavula*
yellow	*dromodromo*

Stationery

book	*ivola*
crayons	*kala*
dictionary	*diksenrī*
exercise book	*'exercise book', pepa ni vuli*
envelope	*wāqanivola*
magazine	*mekesini*

map	*mape*
newspaper	*niusipepa*
pen	*peni*
pencil	*penikau*
scissors	*ikoti*
writing paper	*pepa ni volavola, fulskep*

At the Chemist

baby powder	*pouta*
comb	*iseru*
condoms	*rapa, kodom*
hairbrush	*barasi ni ulu*
razor	*itoro*
razor blade	*batinitoro*
sanitary napkins	*qamuqamu*
soap	*sovu*
talcum powder	*pouta*
toilet paper	*pepa ni valelailai*
toothbrush	*barasi ni bati*
toothpaste	*wainimate ni bati*

Photography

I'd like a film for this camera.	*Dua mada na filimu ni itaba qō.*
How much is it for processing/developing?	*Vica na isau ni sava itaba?*
When will it be ready?	*Siga cava sa na oti kina?*
Do you fix cameras?	*Nī dau sere itaba?*

camera	*itaba*
film	*filimu*
B&W film	*filimu loaloa vulavula*
colour film	*filimu roka*

Smoking

tobacco, cigarettes (generic)	*tavako*
a single cigarette	*itibi*
lighter	*māsese (benisini)*
matches	*māsese*
pipe	*paipo*

A packet of cigarettes, please. *Kerea mada dua na pākete tavako.*

Do you have a light? *Au kere māsese.*

Weights & Measures

gram	*qaramu*
kilogram	*kilo*
pound	*pāudi*
millimetre	*milimita*
centimetre	*sedimita*
metre	*mita*
kilometre	*kilomita*
half a litre	*veimāmā ni lita*
litre	*lita*
inch	*idi*
foot	*fute*
yard	*iyate*
mile	*maile*

SHOPPING

Sizes/Quantities

big	*levu*
bigger	*levu (cake)*
biggest	*levu duadua*
small	*lailai*
smaller	*lailai (sobu)*
smallest	*lailai duadua*
enough	*rauta*
heavy	*bībī*
less	*lailai*
light	*māmada*
a little bit	*vakalailai*
long	*balavu*
many	*levu*
more	*levu (cake)*
much	*vakalevu*
short	*lekaleka*
some	*e sō*
tall	*balavu*
too much/many	*sīvia*

Some Useful Words

backpack	*idrekedreke*
bag	*kato*
battery	*beterī*
bottle	*tavaya*
box	*kāteni*
button	*ibulukau*
candles	*kādrala*
change	*veisau*

discount	*lutusobu*
gold	*koula*
mirror	*iloilo*
needle (sewing)	*icula (ni culacula)*
packet	*pākete*
plastic	*taku*
plastic bag	*palasitika*
receipt	*rīsiti*
silver	*siliva*
thread	*wāniculacula*

Health

All medical personnel speak English, but will feel much better for hearing you attempt to speak Fijian; and if you wish to try the fabled Fijian herbal medicine or massage, you may need to explain your symptoms in Fijian.

I am sick.	*Au tauvimate.*
My friend is sick.	*E tauvimate noqu itōkani.*
I need a doctor.	*Au via raici vuniwai.*
Where can I find a good doctor?	*I vei dua na vuniwai vinaka?*
Could you please call a doctor?	*Qiria mada e dua na vuniwai.*
Do you know a Fijian herbal practitioner?	*O(nī) kilā e dua na vuniwai vakaviti?*
Do you know a Fijian masseur?	*O(nī) kilā e dua na dauveibobo?*

Where is ... ?	*I vei na ...*
a doctor	*vuniwai*
the hospital	*valenibula*
the chemist	*kēmesi*
a dentist	*vuniwai ni bati*

Complaints

I feel dizzy.	*E boiri na mataqu.*
I feel weak.	*Au malumalumu.*

I've been bitten by something.	*Dua na kā sā katī au.*
I'm having trouble breathing.	*Au ceguleka.*
I've been vomiting.	*Au lualua.*
I can't sleep.	*Au sega ni moce rawa.*
I can't move my ...	*E mate na ...*
It hurts here.	*E mosi i kē.*
My ... hurts.	*E mosi na ...*
I have a heart condition.	*E dau leqa na utoqu.*

I have ...	
anaemia	*E maca noqu drā.*
asthma	*Au dau ceguleka/ceno.*
a burn	*Au sā kama.*
constipation	*Au sega ni valelailai rawa.*

a cold	*Au tauvi matetaka.*
a cough	*Au vūvū tiko.*
cramp (of leg)	*E drō na lewe ni yava-qu.*
dengue fever	*Au tauvi deqi*
diarrhoea	*Au coka*
dysentery	*Au tauvi cokadrā*
a fever	*Au tauvi fiva*
food poisoning	*Au gaga*
a headache	*E mosi na uluqu*
indigestion	*E mulo na ketequ*
an infection in my ...	*E vūvūcā na ... qu.*
an inflammation in my ...	*E vuce na ... qu.*
influenza	*Au tauvi matetaka.*
an itch	*Au milamila.*
lice	*Au tauvi lise.*
low/high blood pressure	*E malumalumu/tubu noqu drā.*
malaria	*Au tauvi malāria*
a migraine	*Au tauvi kuita*
mucus	*E bī na ucuqu*
a pain in my ...	*E mosi na ... qu*
a rash on my ...	*E wādadamu na ... qu*
rheumatism	*Au tauvi sasala*
sprain	*Au mavule*
a sore throat	*E mosi noqu itilotilo*
a stomachache	*E mosi na ketequ*
sunburn	*Au kaīsiga*
a swelling in my ...	*E vuce na ... qu*
a temperature	*E katakata na ... yagoqu*
venereal disease	*Au tauvi mate cā*
worms	*Au ukomu*

It's ...	*E ...*
broken	*ramusu*
dislocated	*lutu*
sprained	*mavule*

Some Useful Words & Phrases

I am diabetic.	*Au tauvi matenisuka.*
I am epileptic.	*Au manumanusoni.*
I'm on the pill. (contraceptive)	*Au gunu vuanikau ni yalani.*
I haven't had my period for ... months.	*Sā vula ... sega ni tauvi au na matenivula.*
I have been vaccinated.	*Au sā cula oti.*
I have my own syringe.	*E tiko na noqu icula.*
I'm allergic to penicillin.	*E dau lako vakacā vei au na pēnisilini*

Parts of the Body

See the Grammar chapter, page 25, for how to use the words ending in a hyphen (suffix-possessed). Essentially, 'my arm' is *liga-qu*; 'your arm' is *liga-mu;* 'his/her arm' is *liga-na*, and so on.

ankle	*qurulāsawa*
appendix	*pēdiki*
arm	*liga-*
back	*daku-*
blood	*drā*

bone	*sui*
breast	*sucu-*
chest	*sere-*
ear	*daliga-*
elbow	*duruduruniliga-*
eye	*mata-*
face	*mata-*
finger	*iqāqaloniliga-*
foot	*yava-*
hand	*liga-*
head	*ulu-*
heart	*uto-*
hip	*dibi-*
kidney	*ivi-*
knee	*duru-*
leg	*yava-*
liver	*yate-*
lung	*yatevuso-*
mouth	*gusu-*
muscle	*ua, māsela*
neck	*domo-*
nose	*ucu-*
rib	*saresare-*
shoulder	*taba-*
skin	*kuli-*
spine	*suitū*
stomach	*kete-*
teeth	*bati-*
thigh	*saga-*
throat	*itilotilo*
tongue	*yame-*

At the Chemist

I need something for ...	*Me dua na kā baleta na ...*
How many times a day?	*Vakavica ena dua na siga?*

At the Dentist

Is there a good dentist here?	*Dua na vuniwai ni bati vinaka i kē?*
I have a toothache.	*E mosi na batiqu.*
I don't want it extracted.	*Me kua ni cavu.*
Please give me an anaesthetic.	*Au kerea meu vakamoceri.*

More Useful Words

accident	*vakacalakā*
acupuncture	*veicula vakajaina*
addiction	*rawai*
anti-diarrheal drug	*wai ni coka*
bandage	*ivādreti*
bite	*ikata*
bleeding	*drā*
blood pressure	*tubu ni drā*
blood test	*tauri na drā*
contraceptive	*wai ni yalani*
faeces	*valelailai*
injection	*cula*
injury	*mavoa*
itch	*milamila*
medicine	*wainimate*
menstruation	*matenivula*

HEALTH

nausea	*lomalomacā*
ointment	*iboro*
pus	*nana*
urine	*suasua*
wound	*mavoa*

Times, Dates & Festivals

Days

Monday	*Mōniti*
Tuesday	*Tūsiti*
Wednesday	*Vukelulu*
Thursday	*Lotulevu*
Friday	*Vakaraubuka*
Saturday	*Vakarauwai*
Sunday	*Sigatabu*

Months

January	*Jānueri*
February	*Feperueri*
March	*Maji*
April	*Epereli*
May	*Mē*
June	*Junē*
July	*Julai*
August	*Okosita*
September	*Sepiteba*
October	*Okotova*
November	*Nōveba*
December	*Tīseba*

Dates

What date is it today?	*Kavica ni siga nikua?*
It's 28 June.	*Na ikaruasagavulukawalu ni Junē.*
It's 3 June.	*Na ikatolu ni Junē.*
It's 1 April.	*Na imatai ni Epereli.*

Present

Note that *sigalevu* is from about 10 am to about 3 pm, *yakavi* from about 3 pm till night.

today	*nikua*
this morning	*na mataka nikua*
this afternoon/evening	*na sigalevu/yakavi nikua*
tonight	*na bogi nikua*
this week	*na mācawa qō*
this month	*na vula qō*

this year	*na yabaki qō*
immediately	*sara, vakatotolo*
now	*qō (sara gā)*

Past

yesterday	*nanoa*
day before yesterday	*ena bogi rua, na siga yani yā*
yesterday morning	*na mataka nanoa*
yesterday afternoon/evening	*na sigalevu/yakavi nanoa*
last night	*na bogi*
last week	*na mācawa sā oti*
last month	*na vula sā oti*
last year	*na yabaki sā oti*

Future

tomorrow	*nimataka*
day after tomorrow	*ni bogi rua, na siga yani yā*
tomorrow morning	*mataka nimataka*
tomorrow afternoon/evening	*sigalevu/yakavi nimataka*
next week	*mācawa mai qō*
next month	*vula mai qō*
next year	*yabaki mai qō*

Some Useful Words & Phrases

a while ago	*sā dedē toka*
after	*oti*
always	*dau, tū gā, veigauna*
before	*i liu*
early	*totolo*
everyday	*veisiga*
forever	*tawamudu*

killing time	*mokusiga*
late	*bera*
later on	*mālua*
long ago	*yawa, dedē*
never	*sega vakadua*
not any more	*sega tale*
not yet	*se bera*
recently	*se qai ...*
sometimes	*sō na gauna*
soon	*vakarau*
century	*sentiurī*
day	*siga*
fortnight	*mācawa rua*
month	*vula*
night	*bogi*
week	*mācawa*
year	*yabaki*
... years ago	*... na yabaki sā oti*

Through the Day

sunrise	*cabe na siga*
dawn, very early morning	*mataka lailai*
morning (till about 10 am)	*mataka*
midday/afternoon (10 am to 3 pm)	*sigalevu*
noon	*sigalevu tūtū*
evening	*yakavi*
twilight	*karobo*
sundown	*dromu na siga*
midnight	*bogilevu tūtū*

Seasons

These are not much used in the towns.

summer	*vulaikatakata*
autumn	*vulaimatumatua*
winter	*vulaililiwa*
spring	*vulaitubutubu*
dry season	*vulaisiga*
rainy season	*vulaiuca*
hurricane season	*vulaicagilaba*

Time

Note the reverse order of Fijian time-telling when past the hour: 'A minutes past B' is *sivi na B ina A na minuti*. The order for minutes to, however, is as in English: 'A minutes to B' is *vō e A me B*. The word for 'half past' is *veimāmā ni*, but for 'quarter past' it is '15 minutes', *tinikalima (na minuti)*.

What time is it?	*Sā vica na kaloko?*
It is 1 ...	*Sā dua (na kaloko)*
It is 7 ...	*Sā vitu (na kaloko)*
It is 4.10.	*Sā sivi na vā ina tini (na miniti)*
It is 4.15.	*Sā sivi na vā ina tinikalima (na miniti).*
It is 4.20.	*Sā sivi na vā ina ruasagavulu (na miniti).*
It is 4.30.	*Sā veimāmā ni vā.*
It is 4.40.	*Sā vō e ruasagavulu me lima.*
It is 4.45.	*Sā vō e tinikalima me lima.*

o'clock	*na kaloko*
in the morning	*ina mataka*
in the late morning/early afternoon	*ina sigalevu*
in the evening	*ina yakavi*

Religious & National Festivals

There are many festivals in Fiji, reflecting the varied ethnic and religious make-up of the country. For Fijians, Christmas and Easter are celebrated, but essentially as religious festivals.

Vakatawase

The major secular festival, the celebration for the New Year, begins at midnight on 1 January and goes on until the village chief declares it *tabu* 'forbidden', usually a week or so before the new school year begins. In stark contrast to the usual custom in villages, you can make as much noise as you like during *vakatawase*, and children love staying up late at night (sometimes all night) walking round in groups singing songs and letting out whelps, playing riotous games of hide-and-seek, letting off fireworks and detonating bamboo cannon, and beating the hell out of the village *lali* (hollowed-out log drum), which is at other times strictly forbidden. It is becoming increasingly popular in towns too. A custom peculiar to *vakatawase* is *veisui* (throwing water at each other). Children and young people do it just for fun, but adults are more cautious, since custom demands that they compensate the 'dunkee' by giving them an article of clothing as a *ivaka-māmaca* (something to dry themselves with).

Sōlevu

Fijians hold large gatherings called *sōlevu* for occasions such as funerals and marriages. At some, you may have the good fortune to see *meke* (traditional dances) performed. Show your appreciation by shouting *vinaka* and giving *fakawela* (gifts) – either give dancers, while they are performing, small gifts such as sweets, chewing gum, lengths of printed cloth, or dollar notes, or sprinkle talcum powder or *waiwai* (scented coconut oil) on them.

Adi

Fijians in towns often have fund-raising festivals called *Adi*, in which they sell produce, food, handicrafts etc, and where *meke* are also performed.

If you go to a village, you might be invited to a simple *gunu yaqona* (kava party) or a *taralalā*, an old-style European-type dance with a small local guitar band, where it is usually the women who have to drag the men to the floor. There might be fund-raising functions such as a *kati* (buying playing cards and winning small 'prizes', usually food items, if your card is cut from the pack) or *gunusede*, a riotous affair with much joking where you not only pay for your own kava, but pay to have full cups served to others in friendly rivalry.

Numbers & Amounts

Cardinal Numbers

0	*saiva*
1	*dua*
2	*rua*
3	*tolu*
4	*vā*
5	*lima*
6	*ono*
7	*vitu*
8	*walu*
9	*ciwa*
10	*tini*
11	*tínikadua*
12	*tínikarua*
13	*tínikatolu*
14	*tínikavā*
15	*tínikalima*
16	*tínikaono*
17	*tínikavitu*

18	*tínikawalu*
19	*tínikaciwa*
20	*rúasagavulu*
21	*rúasagavulukadua*
22	*rúasagavulukarua*
30	*tólusagavulu*
31	*tólusagavulukadua*
40	*vāsagavulu*
50	*límasagavulu*
60	*ónosagavulu*
70	*vítusagavulu*
80	*wálusagavulu*
90	*cíwasagavulu*
100	*dua na drau*
101	*dua na drau ka dua*
102	*dua na drau ka rua*
193	*dua na drau cíwasagavulukatolu*
200	*rua na drau*
300	*tolu na drau*
400	*vā na drau*
500	*lima na drau*
600	*ono na drau*
700	*vitu na drau*
800	*walu na drau*
900	*ciwa na drau*
1000	*dua na udolu*
2000	*rua na udolu*
100,000	*dua na drau na udolu*
one million	*dua na milioni*
two million	*rua na milioni*

NUMBERS

May I have eight please?	*Aukerea mada e walu.*
I only asked for three.	*Au ā tukuna gā me tolu.*

With people, the word *lē* is used:

There are four of us.	*Keitou lē vā.*
I have six children.	*Eratou lē ono na luvequ.*

Fractions

¼	*dua na ikavā*
⅓	*dua na ikatolu*
½	*veimāmā*
¾	*tolu na ikavā*

Ordinal Numbers

These are formed by prefixing *ika-* to the cardinal number, eg. *na ikatolu ni vale* 'the third house'.

1st	*imatai*
2nd	*ikarua*
3rd	*ikatolu*
4th	*ikavā*
5th	*ikalima*
6th	*ikaono*
7th	*ikavitu*

8th	*ikawalu*
9th	*ikaciwa*
10th	*ikatini*

Some Useful Words

a little (amount)	*vakalailai*
bundle	*ivesu*
one bundle of taro	*e dua na ivesu dalo*
to count	*wilika*
double	*vakarua-taka*
a dozen	*dua na dāseni*
Enough!	*Rauta!*
few	*e vica*
heap	*ibinibini*
two heaps of mangoes	*e rua na ibinibini maqo*
less	*vakalailai*
a lot	*e levu*
many	*levu*
more	*vakalevu*
once	*vakadua*
a pair	*dua na veisā*
percent	*pasede*
some	*e sō*
too much	*sīvia*
twice	*vakarua*

NUMBERS

Vocabulary

Note For many articles and concepts of Western origin, particularly recently introduced ones, Fijians usually use the English word, with a slightly modified pronunciation. Examples are:

words relating to Western science and technology
(adaptor, alarm clock, automatic, carpet, oxygen, rug, shampoo, tissues, video)
plants & animals
(cactus, herb, peach, plum, zebra)
politics
(democracy, republic, revolution, socialism)
commerce
(credit card, reservation, traveller's cheque)
clothing
(blouse, boot, sandals)
arts & crafts
(actor, art, conductor, jazz, museum)
food & drink
(barbecue, chop, coca-cola, grape, grocery, icecream, omelette, pastry, popcorn, salad, sauce, strawberry, yoghurt)
medicine
(antibiotic, disinfectant, narcotic, prescription, typhus, x-ray)
communications
(airmail, express, postcard, registered mail)

Such words are not included in this vocabulary.

When a hyphen is used with a verb, it means that the part after the hyphen is only used when the verb is transitive. So, the following entry: push – *bili-ga* means that 'push' is *bili*, 'push it' is *biliga*, 'push this car' is *biliga na motokā qō*, and 'push him/her' is *biligi koya*.

When a hyphen is used with a noun, eg back – *daku-*, it means that that noun is suffix possessed, so that 'my back' is *dakuqu*, 'your back' is *dakumu*, 'his/her back' is *dakuna*, and so on (see section on possession in grammatical chapter).

Brackets enclosing Fijian words are for words that are optional, according to context.

A

able – *rawa*
aboard – *i waqa*
about (approx) – *rauta*
above – *i cake, i dela-*
abroad – *mai vālagi*
accept – *ciqoma*
accident – *vakacalakā*
accommodation – *ōtela, icili*
ache – *mosi*
across – (go across) *tākoso-va*,
  (across the road/river) *i tai*

addict – *dau-, manamana-*
  addicted to kava
  *daugunuyaqona,
  manamanayaqona*
administration – *veiliutaki*
admire – *qoroya*
admission – *icurucuru*
admit – *vakadinata*
advantage – *kena vinaka*
adventure – *ilakolako tālei*
advice – *vakasala*
aeroplane – *waqavuka*

afraid – *rere*
afraid of – *rerevaka*
after(wards) – *oti*
afternoon – (till about 3pm) *sigalevu*, (from about three) *yakavi*
again – *tale*
against – (lean against) *ravita*, (be against) *saqata*
age – *yabaki*
agree – *duavata, vakadōnuya*
agriculture – *teitei*
ahead – *i liu*
aid – *veivuke*
air – *cagi*
air-conditioned – *vakabatabatātaki*
airline – *kābani ni waqavuka*
airplane – *waqavuka*
all – *kece, taucoko*
allow – *vakadōnuya*
almost – *vōleka*
alone – *duadua, taudua*
also – *tale gā*
always – *dau, tū gā:* always laughing – *dau dredre, dredre tū gā*
amazing – *veivakadrukai*
ambassador – *mata*
among – (things) *i māliwa ni,* (persons) *māliwai*

ancient – *makawa*
and – *kei, qai*
angry – *cudru*
animal – *manumanu*
another – *dua tale,* (different) *duatani*
answer – (v) *sauma,* (n) *isau*
ant – *qasikālōlō*
antiseptic – *wainimate (ni mavoa)*
any – (a quantity of) *na,* (at random) *dua gā*
apple – *yāpolo*
appointment – *veibuku*
approximately – *vakacācā*
argue – *veibā, veileti*
arid – *dravuisiga*
arm – *liga-*
arrive – *yaco*
ascend – *cabe-ta*
ashamed – *māduā*
ask – *taro-ga*
ask for – *kere-a*
aspirin – *aspirini*
at – *i, mai*
aunt – (mother's younger sister) *tina-lailai,* (mother's older sister) *tina-levu,* (father's sister) *nei*
autumn – *vulaimatumatua*
avocado pear – *pea*

awake – *yadra*
away – *tani*

B

baby – *peipei*, *gonedramidrami*
babysitter – *meimei*
bachelor – *dawai*, (eligible) *cauravou*
back – (n) *daku-*, (be back, come back) *lesu mai*
backpack – *idrekedreke*
bad – *cā*
bag – *kato, taga, beki*
baggage – *iyāyā*
baker – *dauvavimadrai*
balcony – *varada*
ball – *polo*
banana – *jaina*, (cooking) *vudi*
band (musical) – *mataqiriqiri*, (military) *matabani*
bandage – (v) *vādreti-taka*, (n) *i-vādreti*
bank – *baqe*
banknote – *noti, ilavo pepa*
bar – *valenigunu*
bark – (n) *kuli-*, (v) *kodro*
basket – *kato, basikete*

bath – *tavu ni sīsili*
bathe – *sili, sīsili*
bathroom – *valenisili*
bay – *toba*
beach – (landing) *matāsawa*, (bathing) *bāravi nuku*
beans – *bini*
beard – *kumi-*
beautiful – *totoka*
because – *baleta, ni*
bed – *imocemoce, idavodavo*
bedbug – *kutunitana*
beef – *bulumakau*
beer – *bia*
before – *i liu*
beggar – *daukerekere*
begin – *tekivū*
beginner – *se qai vuli*
behind – *i muri, daku-*
  behind you – *i dakumu*
belch – *derekona, todrogē*
believe – *vakabauta*
bell – *lali*
below – *i rā*
bent – *kalove*
beside – *i yasa-*
best – *vinaka duadua*
better – *vinaka (cake)*
between – *i loma ni … kei …*
bible – *ivolatabu*
bicycle – *basikeli*

big – *levu*

bill – *bili*

bird – *manumanu (vuka)*

birthday – *siganisucu*

biscuit – *keke,* (cracker, ship biscuit) *bisikete*

bit – *tiki-*

bitter – *gaga*

black – *loaloa*

blame – *beitaka*

blanket – *vulāqeti*

bleed – *drā*

bless – *vākalougatataka*

blind – *mataboko*

blister – *buta*

blond – *uluvula*

blood – *drā*

blow – (wind) *liwa,* (person) *uvu-ca*

blue – *karakarawa*

board – (v) *vodo*

boat – *waqa, boto*

body – *yago-*

boil – (n) *bō,* (v) *vakasaqa-ra*

boiled – *saqa*

bomb – *bomu*

book – *ivola*

bookshop – *sitoa ni ivola*

bored – *vucesā*

boring – *vakavucesā*

born – *sucu*

borrow – *kerea, vakayagataka*
Please may I borrow your ...
Au kerea/vakayagataka mada nomu ...

boss – *boso*

both – *ruarua*

bottle – *tavaya*

box – *kāteni*

boy – *gonetagane*

boyfriend – *itau (tagane)*

bracelet – *qato*

brave – *yaloqāqā*

bread – *madrai*

breadfruit – *uto*

break – *musuka,* (glass, china) *voroka,* (rope, vine) *gutuva*

break open – *basu-ka*

breakfast – *ikatalau,* (have breakfast) *katalau*

breast – *sucu-*

breastfeed – *vakasucuma*

breathe – *cegu*

breeze – *mudre*

bribe – *vāqumia*

bridge – *wavu*

bright – *ramasē*

bring – *kau-ta mai*

broken – *kamusu,* (bone) *ramusu,* (glass, china) *kavoro*

brother –
  (male's older brother) *tuaka-*,
  (male's younger brother) *taci-*,
  (female's brother) *gāne-*
brown – *braun, raradamu*
bruise – *dābuiloā*
brunet, brunette – *uludamu*
bucket – *vōkete*
bug – *burogo*
build – (building) *tara/tarā*,
  (wall) *tuva/tuvā*, (bridge)
  viri-a
building – *vale*
bull – *tamanibulumakau*
burn – (v) *kama*, (tr) *vākamā*
bus – *basi*
business – *bisinisi*
busy – *osooso, ogaoga*
but – *ia, gā*
butcher – *buja*
butter – *bata*
butterfly – *bēbē*
buy – *voli-a*

C

cabbage – *kāveti*
café – *valenikana*
cake – *keke*
camera – *itaba*
camp – (v) *vakavalelaca*,
  keba, (n – army) *keba*

candle – *kādrala*
candy – *loli*
capital – *korotūraga*
car – *motokā*
cards – (play cards) *veimau*,
  (pack of cards) *imau*
care (to take care of) –
  qarauna, māroroya,
  I don't care.
  Veitālia (vei au).
carpenter – *mātai*
carrot – *kāreti*
carry – *kau-ta*
carry in arms – *roqo-ta*
carry (baby) in arms – *keve-ta*
carry on back – *dreke-ta*
carry (person) on back – *vavā*
carry on shoulder – *cola-ta*
cassava – *tavioka*
cat – *pusi*
catch – (thing thrown) *ciqo-ma*,
  (thing running) *tobo-ka*
catholic – *katolika*
cattle – *bulumakau*
cave – *qaravatu*
cemetery – *ibulubulu*
cent – *sede*
centre – *loma-donu*
certain – *kilā sara gā*
chair – *idabedabe*
chance – *gauna*

VOCABULARY

change (money) – *veisau-taka*
chat – *veitalanoa*
cheap – *saulailai,*
  saurawarawa
cheese – *jisi*
chemist (pharmacy) – *kēmesi*
cheque – *jeke*
chewing gum – *drega*
chicken – *toa*
chief – *tūraga*
chief's house – *valelevu*
child – *gone,* (offspring)
  luve-
chilli – *rōkete, boro*
chocolate – *jokeliti*
choose – *digia*
chop – (v) *taya*
Christmas – *Siganisucu*
Christmas Eve – *Kirisimasivi*
church – *valenilotu*
cigarette – *tavako, itibi*
citizen – *lewenivanua*
city – *siti*
clap with cupped hands –
  cobo
clean – (v) *sava-ta,*
  (adj) *savasavā*
clear – (water) *makare,*
  (message, meaning)
  macala, matata
clever – *vuku*

climb – *kaba-ta*
clock – *kaloko*
close – *sogo-ta*
clothing – *isulu*
cloud – *ō*
coast – *bāravi*
coat – *kote*
cockroach – *kokoroti*
coconut – *niu,* (drinking
  coconut) *bū*
coffee – *kofi*
coin – (silver) *ilavo siliva,*
  (copper) *ilavo varasa*
cold – *liliwa, batabatā*
come – *lako mai*
come and – *mai*
comfortable – (person) *tiko*
  vinaka, (chair) *malumu,*
  dakoba
communist – *komunisi*
company – *kābani*
complex – *vereverea*
comrade – *itōkani*
condom – *rapa, kodom*
congratulations – *vinaka*
  vakalevu
constipation – *qaco ni kete*
contagious – *dewa*
contraceptive – *kā ni yalani*
conversation – *veitalanoa,*
  veivosaki

convict – *kaivesu*

cook – (n) *dauvakasaqa, kuka*, (v) *vakasaqa*, (in earth oven – intr) *vavavi*, (tr) *vavi-a*

cool – *liliwa*

cooperative – (adj) *yalorawarawa*, (society) *isoqosoqo cokovata*

copper – *kopa*

cord – *wā*

corn – *silā*

corned beef – *bulumakau tawaitini*

corner – *kona*, (road) *iwāvoki, ilesu*

correct – *donu*

corrupt – *duka*

cost – (n) *isau*

cotton – (material) *isulu dina*, (plant, cotton wool) *vauvau*

cough – *vū*

cough drop – *loli ni vū*

count – (v) *wiliwili*, (tr) *wilika*

coup – *vuaviri*

court – *mataveilewai*

cousin – *tuaka-, taci-, gāne-, tavale-, dauve-, davola-* (see section in the Small Talk chapter, page 62)

cow – *(tinani)bulumakau*

crab – *qari*, (land crab) *lairo*

crazy – *lialia*

cream – *kirimu*

crooked – *veve*

crop – *itei*

cross – (adj) *rarawa*, (n) (religious) *kauveilatai*, (mark) *kōrosi*

cry – *tagi*

cultivate – (land) *teivaka*, (crop) *tea*

cup – *bilo*

custom – *itovo*

customs – *kasitaba*

cut – (v) (hair, paper) *koti-va*, (bread) *musu-ka*

D

dad – *tā*

daily – *veisiga*

damp – *via suasua, tarasua*, (not yet dry) *kulumaca*

dance – *dānisi*, (traditional) *meke*

dangerous – *rerevaki*

dark – *butō*

date (time) – *tikinisiga*

daughter – *luve- (yalewa)*

dawn – *kida na mataka*
day – *siga*
dead – *mate*
deaf – *dīdīvara*
death – *mate*
decide, decision – *lewā*
deep – *tītobu*
delay – (v) *vakaberā*
delicious – *maleka*
delightful – *tālei*
delirious – *vosavosa*
demonstration (protest) –
    vakaraitaki kudru
dentist – *vuniwai ni bati,*
    dauveicavu
deny – *caki-taka*
depart, departure – *biubiu,*
    gole, lako
descend, descent – *siro*
desert – (v) *drōtaka*
dessert – *ivakalomavinaka*
destroy – *talaraka,*
    vāqeavutaka
detail – *tikina lailai*
detailed – *matailalai*
development –
    veivakatorocaketaki
diarrhoea – *coka ni kete*
die – *mate*
different – *duidui, duatani*
difficult – *drēdrē*

dinner – (midday meal)
    ivakasigalevu, (have
    dinner) *vakasigalevu,*
    (evening meal)
    ivakayakavi,
    (have dinner) *vakayakavi*
direct – *dodonu*
dirt – *qele*
dirty – *duka*
disadvantage – *kena cā*
disagree with – *vakacalā*
discount – *musu, lutusobu*
discover – *kune-a*
discrimination – *veiwasei,*
    veivakaduiduitaki
disease – *mate*
disgusting – *vakasisila*
dish – *disi*
dishonest – *veidābui*
distant – *yawa*
district – *tikina*
dive – (in water) *nunu,* (into
    water) *coka, dokoulu*
do – *caka-va*
doctor – *vuniwai*
dog – *kolī*
doll – *matakau, doli*
dollar – *dola*
don't – *kua (ni)*
door – *kātuba*
double – *taurua*

down – *sobu*
downstairs – *i rā*
downtown – *i lomanitāuni*
dream – *tadra*, (tr) *tadrā*
dress – (v) *vakaisulu-taka*,
　(n) *vinivō*
dried – *vakamāmacataki*, (in
　the sun) *sigani*
drink – (n) *gunu*, *wainigunu*
　(v) *gunu-va*
drinkable (water) – *vinaka*
drive – *draiva-taka*
driver – *draiva*
drug – *wai*
dry – *māmaca*
duck – *gā*
during – *ni*
dust – (n) *kuvu*, (v) *qusiqusi*,
　(tr) *qusi-a*

E

each – *yā-*, *dui*
　We had one each.
　　Keitou yādua.
　Let's each go to our respec-
　tive rooms.
　　Tou dui lako i nona rumu.
ear – *daliga-*
early – (not late) *totolo*,
　(early in the day)
　vakamataka

earn – *rawata*
earnings – *ilavo e rawa(ta)*
earring – *sau*
earth – (soil) *qele*, (world)
　vuravura
earth oven – *lovo*
earthquake – *uneune*
east – *isi*
east wind – *tokalau*
Easter weekend –
　Siganimate
Easter Sunday – *Siga ni
　Tucaketale*, (Catholic)
　Pāseka
easy – *rawarawa*
eat – *kana*, (tr) *kania*
economic – *vakailavo*
economy – *bula vakailavo*
education – *vuli*
egg – *yaloka*
eggplant – *baigani*
elbow – *duruduruniliga-*
elder – *qase*
election – *veidigidigī*
electricity – *livaliva*
embarrassed, embarrassment
　– *māduā*
embarrassing – *vakamāduā*
embassy – *valenivolavola*,
　ebesī
employee – *vakailesilesi*

employer – *solicakacaka, itaukei ni cakacaka*

empty – *lala*, (of liquid) *maca*

end – (n) *mua-, itinitini*, (v) *oti, tini*

energy – *icegu, igū*

English – *vosa vakavālagi*

enjoy (oneself) – *mārau*

enough – *rauta*

enter – *curu*

entry – *icurucuru*

envelope – *waqanivola*

equal – *tautauvata*

Equator – *ekuata*

evening – *yakavi*

event – (gathering) *soqo*

ever – *bau*

every – *kece*

everyone – (all of them) *ira kece*, (all of us) *keda kece*

everything – *kā kece*

excellent – *uasivi*

exchange – (v) *veisau-taka*

exhausted – *wawale, dadaga*

exile – *tū tani*

exotic – *kau tani mai*

expensive – *saulevu*

experience – (v) *tovolea*

export – (v) *vākau-ta i vanuatani*

eye – *mata-*

F

face – *mata-*

fair – (hair) *damu*, (just) *dodonu*

faithful – *yalodina*

fall (v) – (drop) *lutu*, (fall over) *bale*, (rain) *tau*

false – *lasu*

family – *vūvale*

fan – *iri*, (electric) *irinicagi*

far – *yawa*

fare – *ivodovodo*

farm – (v) *teitei*, (n) *iteitei*

farmer – *dauteitei*

fast – *totolo*

fast (not eat) – *lolo*

fat – (adj) *levulevu*, (n) *uro*

father – *tama-*

fault – *cala*

fear – *rere-vaka*

fee – *isau*

feel – (with hand) *tarā*, (emotion) *loma-*

feeling – *loma-*

female – (n) *yalewa*, (adj) *vakayalewa, ni yalewa*

feminine – *vakayalewa*

fence – *bā, bai*

ferry – (v) *vakaleleca*, (n) *waqa ni vakalele*, (take a ferry) *lele* fertile – *bula*

festival – *soqo, adi*

fever – *katakata, fiva*

few – *vica*

field – *rārā*, (planted) *iteitei*

fight – *veivala*

Fiji – *Viti*

Fijian – (person) *kai Viti, itaukei*, (language) *(vosa) vakaviti*
What's the Fijian for ...?
A cava na vakaviti ni ... ?

fill – *vakasīnaita*

film – (cinema) *iyaloyalo*, (camera) *filimu*

find – *kunea*

fine (good) – *daumaka*

fine (penalty) – *itotogi*

finger – *iqāqaloniliga-*

finished – *oti*

fire – *kama*

firewood – *buka*

first – *imatai*

fish – (n) *ika*, (v) *qoli*, (with line) *siwa*

flag – *kuila*

flat – *tautauvata*

flea – *kutu*

flesh – *lewe-, viciko*

flight – *vuka*

flip-flops – *(ivāvā) sabisabi*

flood – *wāluvu*

floor – *fuloa*

floor (storey) – *taba-*
on the 1st (American 2nd)
floor – *ena tabarua*

flour – *falawa*

flower – (generic) *senikau*, (specific) *se-*
mango flower – *senimaqo*

fly – (v) *vuka*, (n) *lago*

follow – *muri-a*

food – *kākana*

for – *ni* (see also Possession in the Grammar chapter, page 25)

forbid – *vakatabuya*

forbidden – *tabu*

force – (n) *igū*

foreign – *ni vanuatani*

foreigner – *kaitani*

forest – *veikau*

forget – *guileca-va*

forgive – *vosota*

fork – (eating) *icula*, (garden) *mataivā*

fragile – *kakavorovoro rawarawa*

freckle – *digo*

free (of charge) – *soli wale*
free (not bound) – *galala*
fresh (not stale) – *qai buta*, (fruit) *bulabula*
fried – *tavuteke*
friend – *itau, ilālā, kābani*
We are friends.
Keirau veitau.
friendly – *yalololoma*
from – *i, mai*
front – *mata-*
frozen – *cevata*
fruit – *vuanikau*
fry – (v) *tavuteke-taka*
full – *sīnai*, (after eating) *mamau*
fun – *lasa*
funny – *lasa*
furniture – *iyāyā ni vale*

G

game – *qito*
garbage – *benu*
garden – *iteitei*
garlic – *qāliki*
gate – *matamata*
generous – *lomasoli*
gentle – *yalomālua*
gentleman – *tūraga*
gently – *vakamālua*

get – (obtain) *rawata*, (become) *sā ... mai*
It's getting cold.
Sā liliwa mai.
get off – *sobu*
get on – *vodo*
girl – *goneyalewa*
girlfriend – *itau (yalewa)*
give – *solia*
give back – *vakasukā*
glass (of water) – *bīloiloilo*
glasses – *matailoilo*
gloves – *qaniliga*
go – *lako*, (by vehicle) *vodo*
go ahead – *liu*
go and – *lai*
go back – *lesu*
goat – *mē*
God – *Kalou*
gold – *koula*
good – *vinaka*
good at – *mātai*: good at games – *mātai na qito*, good at Fijian – *mātai na vosa vakaviti*
government – *matanitū*
grandchild – *makubu-*
grandfather – *tuka-*
grandmother – *bu-*
grass – *cō*
grease – *qirisi*

greedy – *kocokoco*
green – *drokadroka*
greet – *kidavaka*
grind – *qaqi-a*
grow – *tubu*, (tr) *tei*
guava – *quawa*
guess – (v) *vākilakilā*
guide – (v) *vakasalataka*,
   (by the hand) *tubera*
guilty – *yaloveivutuni*
guitar – *qitā*
gun – *dakai*

H

hair – *ulu-*, *drauniulu-*
half – *veimāmā*
hand – *liga-*
handbag – *beki*, *bāusi*
handicraft – *cakacaka ni liga*
handkerchief – *itāvoi*
handsome – *rairaivinaka*,
   musudonu
happen – *yaco*
happy – *mārau*, (contented)
   vakacegu, *yalovakacegu*
hard – (not soft) *kaukaua*,
   (not easy) *drēdrē*, (try,
   work, look) *matua*
hardworking – *mākutu*
hat – *isala*

hate – *cata, sēvaka*
head – *ulu-*
headache – *mosi ni ulu*
healed – (wound) *mavo*,
   (disease) *bula*
health – *bula*
healthy – *bulabula*
hear – *rogoca*
heart – *uto-*
heat – *katakata*
heavy – *bībī*
help – *veivuke*, (tr) *vukea*
   It helps.
   E yaga.
hen – *(tinani)toa*
here – *i kē*
heron – *belō*
hibiscus – *senitoa*
hiccup – *macedru*
high – *rewa, yawa i cake*
hill – *delana*
hit – (strike) *moku-ta*,
   (target) *lau-ta*
hitchhike – *tātaro motokā*
hold – *taura*
hole – *qara*
holiday – (government)
   olodei, (not at school)
   sereki, (not at work) *livi*,
   (trip) *gādē*
holy – *tabu*

home – *vale*
homesick – *vakanānanu*
homosexual – (male) *vakasālewalewa*, (inf) *qaurī, pufta*, (female) *daukauyalewa*, (inf) *les*
honest – *yalodina*
hope – *nuitaka*
horse – *ose*
hospitable, hospitality – *veiciqomi*
hot – *katakata*
hotel – *ōtela*
hour – *awa*
house – *vale*
housework – *sāsāmaki*
how – *vakacava*
how much/many – *vica*
hug – (v) *veimoko*, (tr) *mokota*
human – *tamata*
hungry (to be) – *viakana*
hurricane – *cagilaba*
hurry (to be in a) – *vakatotolo*
hurry up! – *totolo!*
hurt – (injured) *mavoa*, (ache) *mosi*, (tr) *vakararawataka*, *vakamavoataka*
husband – *wati- (tagane)*

I

ice – *aisi, waicevata*
idea – *vākāsama*
idiot – *lialia*
if – *kē, kēvakā*
ill – *tauvimate*
illegal – *tabu (vakalawa)*
immediately – *sara*
imitate – *vakamuria*
imitation – *ivakatākarakara*
import – (v) *vākau-ta mai (vanuatani)*
impossible – *sega ni rawa* (often sounds like 'sedrawa' in rapid speech)
imprison – *vesu-ka*
in – *i, mai*
incident – *kā e yaco*
include – (v) *wili kina*
inconvenient – *drēdrē*
increase – (v) *tubu*, (tr) *vakatubura*
Indian – (n) *kai Idia*, (adj) *vakaidia*
indigestion – *mulo ni kete*
individual – *tamata yādua*
indoors – *i lomanivale*
industry – (manufacturing) *buliyāyā*, (tourist) *cakacaka ni saravanua*

infected – *vūvūcā*
infectious – *dewa*
information – *itukutuku*
injection – (have an) *cula*, (give an) *veicula*, (tr) *culā*
injury – *mavoa*
insect – *manumanu (lailai)*
insect repellant – *ivana ni manumanu*
inside – *i loma*
insurance – *inisua*
insure – *inisua-taka*
intelligent – (thinking) *vakayalo*, (clever) *vuku*, *uluvinaka*
interested in – *tāleitaka*
interesting – *tālei*
international – *ni veimatanitū*
invitation – *veisureti*
invite – *sureta*
iron – (n) (metal) *kaukamea*, (clothes) *vatu (ni yayani)*
iron – (v) *yayani*, (tr) *yani-a*, *yayani-taka*
island – *yanuyanu*
itch – *milamila*

J

jacket – *jākete*
jail – *valeniveivesu*
jar – *tavaya*

jewellery – *iukuuku (vatu tālei)*
job – (employment) *cakacaka*, (task) *itavi*
joke – *veiwali*
journalist – *dauvolaitukutuku*
judge – *tūraganilewā*
juice – (generic) *wainimoli*, (specific) *waini-*
guava juice – *wainiquawa*
jug – *joke*, (electric) *kuronitī livaliva*
jump – *lade*, *rika*
jumper/sweater – *siqileti (ni katakata)*
jungle – *veikauloa*
just – *gā*, (recently) *se qai*
justice – *dodonu*

K

kava – *yaqona*
kava root – *waka*
kava bowl – *tānoa*
keen – *mākutu*
kerosene – *karasini*
key – *kī*
kick – *caqe-ta*
kidney – *ivi*
kill – *vakamatea*, (animal) *moku-ta*

kilogram – *kilo*
kilometre – *kilomita*
kind – (n) *mataqali:* a kind
   of food – *na mataqali
   kākana,* (adj) *yalovinaka,
   yalololoma*
kindergarten – *kida*
kiss – *kisi-va,* (in Fijian
   fashion, cheek-to-cheek)
   regu-ca
kitchen – *valenikuro*
knapsack – *idrekedreke*
knee – *duru-*
knife – *isele*
know – *kilā*

L

lace – *talitali,* (shoelace)
   wā(ni ivāvā)
lady – *marama*
lake – *drano*
lamb – *lami*
lamp – *cina*
land – (n) *vanua, qele,* (v) *tau*
landslide – *sisi na qele*
language – *vosa*
last – (v) not translated
   It lasts a week.
   E mācawa dua.

last (adj) – *iotioti, imurimuri,*
   (week, month) *sā oti*
late – (not early) *bera,* (late
   in the day) *vakabogi*
laugh – *dredre*
laundry – (dirty clothes)
   isulu duka, (room)
   valenisavasava
law – *lawa*
lawyer – *loya*
lazy – *vucesā*
leader – *iliuliu*
learn – *vuli-ca*
leather – *leca,
   kulinimanumanu*
left – *imawī*
left-wing – *tai mawī*
leg – *yava-*
legal – *vakalawa*
lemon – *moli karokaro*
Lent – *lede*
less – *lailai*
letter – *ivola*
lettuce – *lētisi*
liar – *tamata lasulasu*
library – *valenivola,
   valeniwilivola*
lie – (down) *davo,* (tell a)
   lasu
life – *bula*
lift (elevator) – *liva*

light – (n) *cina*,
  (adj) (not heavy) *māmada*,
  (not dark) *rārama*,
  (v) – (fire, cigarette)
  tutuvaka, tugia
lighter – (cigarette) *māsese*
  (benisini)
like (similar) – *vakā*
like – (v) *tāleitaka, maleka*
  I like sailing – *Au tāleitaka*
  na soko/E maleka vei au
  na soko
lime – *moli laini*
line – *iyatu, laini*
lip – *tebenigusu-*
lipstick – *iboronigusu*
listen – *vakarorogo*, (to)
  rogoca, vakarogoca
little – *lailai*, (a little)
  vakalailai
live – (v) *bula*, (reside)
  vakaitikotiko
lizard – *moko*
load – (n) *iusana*,
  (v) *vakavodo-ka*
lobster – *urau*, (mangrove)
  manā
lock – (n) *loka*
lolly (sweet) – *loli*
long – *balavu*, (time) *dedē*
look – *rai*, (at) *raica*

look for – *vāqarā*
lorry – *lori*
lose – *yali*
  I've lost my purse.
  Sā yali na noqu bāosi.
lose (not win) – *druka, lusi*
loud – *rogolevu*
love – (child) *lomana*, (adult)
  domona, mateca
low – *rewairā, lōlovirā*
luck, lucky – *kalougata*
luggage – *iyāyā*
lump (swelling) – *vuce*
lunch – *ivakasigalevu*, (have
  lunch) *vakasigalevu*
lungs – *yatevuso*
luxury – (live in) *tiko vinaka*,
  (idle) *kanamoce*

M

machine – *mīsini*
mad – *lialia, matiruku*
made (to be made of) – *buli*
  mai na
magazine – *mekesini*
maid – *dauveiqaravi*
majority – *lewelevu*
make – *caka-va*, (shape, manufacture) *buli-a*
make sure – *vakadeitaka*

make-up – *sāsāuni*
She's making herself up.
E sāuni koya tiko.
male – (n) *tagane*, (adj)
vakatagane, ni tagane
man – *tagane (levu)*
manager – *manidia*
mango – *maqo*
mangrove – *dogo, tiri*
mangrove swamp – *veidogo,
veitiri*
many – *levu*
map – *mape*
marble – *māpolo*
market – *mākete*
marriage – *vakamau*
married – *vakawati*
marry – *vakamau-taka*
massage – *veibobo, veimasi,*
(tr) *bobo-ka, masi-a*
mat – *ibe*
matches – *māsese*
matter – (it doesn't matter)
veitālia
mattress – *meteresi*
mature – *matua*
maybe – *dē, beka*
Maybe he's gone.
Dē sā lako/Sā lako beka.
mean – (adj) *yalodrēdrē,
māmāqī*, (v) *ibalebale*

What does ... mean? –
Cava na ibalebale ni ... ?
meat – *lewenimanumanu*
mechanic – *mekeniki*
medicine – *wai, wainimate*
meet – (intentional) *tāvaka*,
(accidental) *sota (kei)*
melon – *mēleni*
mend – (patch) *botana*, (fix)
ripea-taka
menu – *ivolanikana*
message – *itukutuku*
metal – *kaukamea*
midday – *sigalevu tūtū*
middle – *veimāmā*
midnight – *bogilevu tūtū*
mile – *maile*
milk – *sucu*
mind – (n) *loma-, vākāsama*,
(v) *cā vei*
I don't mind.
E sega ni cā vei au.
minister (religious) – *italatala*
minute – *miniti*
mirror – *iloilo*
miss (feel absence of) –
vakanānanu vei, misi-taka
miss (fail to hit, meet, see
etc) – *cala-ta*
mistake – *cala*
mix – (v) *waki-a*, (kava) *lose-a*

mixed – *veiwaki*
modern – *vou, ni gauna qō*
money – *ilavo*
mongoose – *manivusi/
   manipusi*
monkey – *maqe*
month – *vula*
moon – *vula*
more – *levu (cake)*
morning – *mataka*
mother – *tina-*
mountain – *ulunivanua*
mouth – *gusu-*
move (agitate) – *yāvala*,
   (tr) *yāvalata*
move (along) – *toso*,
   (tr) *tosoya*
movie – *iyaloyalo*
mud – *sōsō*
muddy – *sōsō*, (water) *vuvu*
mum – *nā, nānā*
mutton – *māteni*

N

name – *yaca-*
   What's your name?
   O cei na yacamu?
nature – (environment)
   veikābula, (character)
   roka, itovo
near – *vōleka*

neat – *maqosa*
necessary – *yaga, gadrevi*
neck – *domo-*
necklace – *itaube*
needle – *icula(liga)*
neither – *sega (ni dua)*
net – *lawa*
never – *sega vakadua (ni)*
new – *vou*
news – *irogo*
newspaper – *niusipepa, pepa*
next – *tarava*
next (week, month, year) –
   mai qō
   next month – *vula mai qō*
nice – *vinaka, totoka*
night – *bogi*
nightclub – *vālenidānisi*
no – *sega*
noise – *rorogo*
noisy – *kosakosā, rogolevu*
none – *sega (ni dua)*
noon – *sigalevu tūtū*
north – *noca*
north wind – *vualiku*
nose – *ucu-*
not – *sega ni*
not yet – *se bera (ni)*
nothing – *sega (ni dua na
   kā)*, (do nothing) *wele,
   vakasavuliga*

now – *qō, sā*
I'm retired now.
Au sā vakacegu qō.
nurse – *nasi*
nut – no generic term,
classed as *vuanikau* 'fruit';
(specific) *vua-*
Barringtonia nut) *vuanivutu*

O

obvious – *macala*
occupy (live in) – *tawana*
occupy (keep busy) –
vakaogā
occupation (job) – *cakacaka*
ocean – *wasawasa*
odour – *iboi*
offend – *cala*
offer – (v) (volunteer) *bolebole*,
(gift, price) *via solia*
office – *valenivolavola, ōfisi*
officer – (employee)
vakailesilesi, (police)
tūraganiovisa, (army)
tūraganivalu
often – *vakalevu, wāsomā*
oil – *waiwai*
ointment – *iboro*
old – (person) *qase*, (thing)
makawa
old man – *kenatūraga*

old lady – *kenamarama*
on – *i (dela ni)*
once – (not twice) *vakadua*,
(formerly) *i liu*
one – *dua*
onion – *varasa*
only – (wale) *gā*
only one – *dua (wale) gā*
open – (v) *dolava*,
(adj) – *dola*
opinion – *rai, nanuma*
opportunity – *dōnuya*
If I get the opportunity.
Keu dōnuya.
opposite – *veibāsai, i tai*
or – *se*
orange – *moli taiti*,
(mandarin) *maderini*
order – (command) *vakarota*,
(supplies, food) *ota-taka*
order – (n) (command)
ivakarō, (sequence)
veitarataravi
ordinary – *wale*
organisation – *isoqosoqo*
organise – (v) *tuvā, tuvalaka*
original – (authentic) *mai
logana*, (different) *duatani*
other – *e dua*
the other one – *koya e dua*
out – *i tuba*

outside – *i tuba*
over – (finished) *oti*
overboard – *i wai*
overnight – *moce*
overseas – *vanuatani, vālagi*
owe – *dinau (vei)*
own – *taukena*
owner – *itaukei*
oyster – *dio*

P

package – *ioloolo*
packet – *pākete*
padlock – *loka, iviqāqā*
page – *tabana*
pain, painful – *mosi*
painter – *dauboroboro*
pair – *veisā*
palace – *valenitui*
pancake – *panikeke (waicala)*
pants – (trousers) *tarausese*,
    (underwear) *isuluiloma*,
    (inf) *sapo*
paper – *pepa*
parallel – *veidōnui, cici vata*
parcel – *ioloolo*
pardon – *vosota*,
    What was that? – *Ō?*
parents – *itubutubu*
park – (n) *rārā*

park – (v) *kele*, (tr) *vākelea*
parrot – *koki*, (Fijian) *kakā*
part – (n) *tiki-*, (v) (leave
    each other) *veitalatala*,
    (hair) *tawase*
participate – *vakaitavi*
particular – (one) *e dua*,
    (fussy) *digidigi*
parting – (leaving each other)
    veitalatala, (hair) *tawase*
party – *soqo, pati*, (political)
    itō, isoqosoqo
pass – *sīvia*, (ball) *soli-a*,
    pasi-taka
passenger – *pasidia*
passport – *pasipote*
past – *sivi*
path – *sala*
patient – *yalovosota*
pawpaw (papaya) – *weleti*
pay – (v) *sauma*, (n) *isau*
peas – (salted as a snack) *bini*
peace – *vakacegu, sautū*
peanut – *pinati*
pear – *pea (ni vālagi)*
pearl – *mataniciva*
pedestrian – *taubale tiko*
peel – (with fingers) *voci-a*,
    (with knife) *civi-ta*
pen – *peni*
pencil – *penikau*

people – *tamata*
pepper – *pepa*
per – *yā-, dua*
    Two dollars per person.
    Yārua na dola.
    50 dollars per day.
    Limasagavulu na dola dua
    na siga.
percentage – *pasede*
perfect – *totoka vakaoti,*
    tabucala
perhaps – *dē, beka*
permanent – *tūdei*
permission – *veivakadōnui*
permit – (v) *vakadōnuya,*
    (n) *ivolatara*
persecute – *vakararawataka*
persecution –
    veivakararawataki
person – *tamata*
personal – *vakaitaukei*
personality – *yalo-,*
    (well-known person)
    tamata rogo
perspire – *buno*
petrol – *benisini*
pharmacy – *kēmesi*
phone – *qiri*
photo – *itaba*
picnic – *pikiniki,*
    vakatākakana

pie – *pai*
piece – *tiki-*
pig – *vuaka*
pill – *vuanikau*
pillow – *ilokoloko*
pillowcase – *waqanilokoloko*
pilot – *pailate*
pine – *paini*
pineapple – *vaināviu*
pink – *piqi*
pipe – *paipo, vaivo*
place – (n) *vanua*
place – (v) *vakatikora,*
    vakatokara, biuta
plane – (air) *waqavuka,*
    (level land) *bucabuca*
plant – (n) *kau,* (v) *teitei,*
    (tr) *tea*
plastic – *taku*
plastic bag – *palāsitika*
plate – *veleti*
play – (v) *qito,* (guitar,
    drums) *qiri-a,* (piano)
    taba-ka, (on stage) *drama,*
    (play cards) *veimau*
plea – *vakamamasu,*
    (tr) *masu-ta*
please – *mada*
    Please don't.
    Kua mada.
plenty – *levu, talavō*

plug – (sink) *isogo*, (stopper) *isoso*, (electric) *palaka*

plumber – *palama*

pocket – *taga*

poet – *dauniserekali*

point – *dusi-a*

police – *ovisa*

politics – *politiki*

pool – (swimming) – (natural) *tobu ni sīsili, isilisili*

poor – (not rich) *dravudravua*, (unfortunate) *vakaloloma*

positive – *kilā deivaki*

possible – *rawa*

postbox – *katonimeli*

post office – *positōvesi*

postage – *isau ni sitaba*

postage stamp – *sitaba*

pot – *kuro*

potato – *pateta*

pottery – *tulituli*

pound – (weight) *bībī*, (crush) *tuki-a, vutu-ka*

poverty – *dravudravua*

power – (strength) *kaukaua*, (authority) *lewā*, (electric) *livaliva*

practical – *cakacakataki, vakavotukana*

pray, prayer – *masu*

prefer – *vinaka (cake) vei*
I prefer this hotel.
Vinaka (cake) vei au na ōtela qō.

pregnant – *bukete*

prepare – *vakarautaka*

present – (time) *qō*
(gift) – *iloloma*

president – *peresitedi*

pressure – *bī*

pretty – *totoka*, (person) *matamalumu, matavinaka*

prevent – *tārova*

price – *isau*

pride – (have pride in) *cibitaka*, (take pride in) *sakitaka*, (vanity) *dokadokā*

priest – *bete*

Prime Minister – *Paraiminisitā, iLiuliu ni Matanitū*

prison – *valeniveivesu*

prisoner – *kaivesu*, (war) *bōbula*

private – *vakaitaukei*, (have a private conversation) *veivosaki taurua*

probably – *rairai*

problem – *leqa*

process – (v) *cakacaka-taka*, (raw material) *qaqi-a*

procession – *veitarataravi*, *veituitui*, (religious) *porōsesiō*

produce – (show) *vakaraitaka*, (manufacture) *buli-a*

professional – *saumi*, *kenadau*

profit – *tubu*

promise – *yalayala*, (tr) *yalataka*

property – (wealth) *iyau*, (land) *qele*

proportion – (in proportion) *veiraurau*

prostitute – *saqamua*, (at the docks) *kabawaqa*

protect – *taqomaka*

protest – *kudru-vaka*

province – *yasana*

public – (public property) *taukeni rāraba*, (speak in public) *vosa i matanalevu*

pull – *drē*, (tr) *dreta*

punish – *totogi-taka*

pure – (nothing but) *wale* (*gā*), *botoboto* (not soiled) *savasavā*

purple – *lokaloka*

pus – *nana*

push – *bili-ga*

put – *biu-ta*, *toka-ra*

put off (light) – *boko-ca*

put on – (clothes) *dara, vaka*, (radio) *dola-va*, (light) *waqaca*

put out (fire) – *boko-ca*

Q

quality – *vinaka, uasivi*

quarrel – *veibā, veileti*

question – *taro*

quick – *totolo*

quiet – (person) *galugalu*, (place) *vakadīrorogo*

R

rabbit – *rāvete*

race – (of people) *matatamata*, (contest) – *veitau*

racism – *veicati vakamatatamata*

radio – *rētiō, wālesi*

railroad – *sala ni sitima*

rain – *uca*

raincoat – *koteniuca*

rainy – *ucauca*

rape – *kucu-va*

rare – *tūtūyādua*

rat – *kalavo*

raw – (uncooked) *droka*, (unprocessed) *qāqā*

razor – *itoro*

razor-blade – *batinitoro*

read – *wilivola*, (tr) *wilika*

ready – *vakarau*

real – *dina*

realise – *qai kilā*

reason – *vu-*

receipt – *risiti*

receive – *ciqoma, taura*

recent – *vou*

recognise – (person) *kilā na mata-*

recommend – (person) *cavuta*, (action) *vakasala-taka*

record – *katokatoni*, (tr) *katona*

red – *damudamu*

reef – *cakau*

reflection – *iyaloyalo*

refresh – *vakabulabula-taka*

refrigerator – *katoniwaililiwa, firiji*

refugee – *isēnivalu*

refund (v) – *vakasukā*

refuse – *bese-taka*

region – *yasayasa*

regret – *rarawa-taka*

regulation – *lawa*

relation – *weka-*

relationship – *veiwekani*

relax – *vakacegu*

religion – *lotu*

remember – *nanuma*

remote – *yawa*

rent – (n) *isau ni rede*, (v) *rede-taka*

repair – *ripea-taka*, (stitch) *culā*, (patch) *botana*

repeat – *vakarua-taka*

repellent – *ivana (ni manumanu)*

reply – (n) *isau*, (v) *sauma*

report – (v) *tukutuku*

represent – *matataka*

representative – *mata*

republic – *ripabuliki*

request – *kerekere*, (tr) *kerea*

require – *gadreva*

respect – *dokā*

responsibility – *itavi, lewā*

rest – (v) *cegu, vakacegu*, (n) *vō*

restaurant – *valenikana*

retire – *vakacegu*

return – (v) *lesu (mai/yani)*

rhythm – *itautau*

rice – *raisi*

rich – *vutuniyau*

ride – *vodo-ka*
right – (opposite of left) *imatau* (not wrong) – *donu*
right wing – *tai matau*
ring – (n) *mama*, (v) *qiri*
ripe – *dreu*
risk – (n) *vakarerevaki*, (v) *tovolea, bolea*
risk one's life – *bole mate*
river – *uciwai*
river mouth – *gusuniwai*
road – *gaunisala*
roast – (in oven) *vavia*, (over fire) *tavuna*
roasted – (in oven) *vavi*, (over fire) *tavu*
rob – *butako-ca*
robber – *daubutako*
robbery – *butako*
rock – *vatu*
roof – *dela-(nivale)*
room – *rumu*
root – *waka-*, (cause) *vu-*
rope – *dali*
rose – *rosi*
rotten – *cā*, (wood) *vuca*
round – *moqimoqili*
rubbish – *benu*
rugby football – *rakavī*
rule – *lewā*
run – *cici*

S

sacred – *tabu*
sad – *rarawa, lomabībī*
safe – (n) *sefi*, (adj) (put away) *māroroi*, (looked after) *tawani*, (not dangerous) *vinaka*
Is this a safe place to swim?
Vanua vinaka ni qalo qō?
safety – *qaqarauni*
sail – (n) *laca*, (v) *soko*
sailor – *dausoko*
saint – *santo* (m), *santa* (f)
sale – *lutusobu*
salt – *māsima*
same – *tautauvata*
sand – *nuku*
sandwich – *seniwiji*
satisfied – *vakacegu na yalo*, (enough to eat) *mamau*
saucepan – *sosipani*
sausage – *sōseti*
save – (keep) *māroroya*, (not spend) *vakabulā*, (someone's life) *vakabulā*
say – *kaya, tukuna*
scarf – *sikavu*
school – *koronivuli*, (go to school) *vuli*
scissors – *ikoti*
score – *kai*, (a try) *sikoa*

sea – *waitui*, (at sea) *soko tiko*
seagull – *drē, icō*
seasick – *loloa*
seat – *idabedabe*
second – *ikarua*
secret – (adj) *vuni*, (n) *kā lō*
secretary – *vunivola*
section – *tabana*
see – *rai-ca*
see off – *talaca*
seed – *sore-*
selfish – *kocokoco*
sell – *volitaka*
seller – *(dau)volivolitaki*
send – (thing) *vākau-ta*, (person) *talā*
separate – *wase-a*
serious – *bībī*
servant – *italai, dauveiqaravi*
settle – (reside) *tiko vakadua*, (bird) *rō*
several – *vica*
sew – *culacula*, (tr) *culā*
shady – *rurugu*
shake – *kurekure*, (tr) *kurea*
shake hands – *lūlulu*
shallow – *mātia, vōdea*
shape – (n) *vatuķa-, ibulibuli*, (v) *buli-a*
  What shape is it?
  E buli vakacava?

share – (n) *ivota, iwase*, (company) *sea*, (v) *votā, wasea*
shark – *qiō*
shave – *torotoro*, (tr) *toro-ya*
sheep – *sipi*
sheet – *siti*
shell – (seashell, generic) *qanivivili*, (specific) *qa-* clam shell – *qanivāsua*
ship – *waqa*, (cruise) *meli*
shirt – *sote*
shoe – *ivāvā*
shoot – *vana*, (tr) *vanā*
shop – *sitoa*
shore – *bāravi*
short – *leka, lekaleka*
shortage – *leqa*
shout – *kaila*, (buy drinks etc) *saute*
show – (v) *vakaraitaka*
shower – *sawa*
shrimp – *moci*
shut – *sogo-ta*
shut up! – *tiko lō!*
shy – *māduā*
sick – *tauvimate*
sickness – *mate*
side – *yasa-*
sight (view) – *irairai*

sign – *saini*
silent – (person) *galugalu*, (place) *vakadīrorogo*
silk – *silika*
silver – *siliva*
similar – *mataqali vata, vakā*
simple – *rawarawa*
sin – (v) *valavalacā*, (n) *ivalavalacā*
since – (because) *me vakā ni*, (time) *se*
I've been waiting since five. *Au se wāwā tiko ena lima.*
sing – *laga-ta, sere*
single (unique) – *duadua* (unmarried – *dawai*)
sir – *saka*
I have come to see you, sir. *Au lako saka tiko mai.*
sister – (female's older sister) *tuaka-*, (female's younger sister) *taci-*, (male's sister) *gāne-*, (nurse, religious) *sisitā*
sit – *dabe*
situation – *vanua, itūtū*
size – *levu, saisi*
skin – *kuli-*
skirt – *liku*
sky – *lomālagi*
slap – *sabi-ca, saba-ka*

sleep – *moce*
sleepy (to be) – *viamoce*
slender – *tololailai*
slow – (too slow) *berabera*, (nice and slow) *mālua*
slowly – *vakamālua*
small – *lailai*
smart (clever) – *mātai*
smell (n) – *iboi*, (v) *boi*, (tr) *boica*
smile – *dredre*
smoke (n) – *kubou*, (v) *vakatavako*
snake – *gata*
sneeze – *suru*
snow – *uca cevata*
soap – *sovu*
sober – *bula vinaka*
soccer – *soka*
sock – *sitōkini*
soft – *malumu*, (sound) *rogolailai*
soil – *qele*
soldier – *sōtia*
solid – *qāqā*
some – (e) *sō*
somebody – (e) *dua*
something – (e) *dua na kā*
sometimes – (e) *sō na gauna*
son – *luve-* (tagane)
song – *sere*

soon – *vakarau, vōleka*
It'll soon be open.
Sā vakarau dola.
It'll soon be finished.
Sā vōleka ni oti.
sorry – (I am) *vosoti au,*
(feel sorry for) *lomana*
soul – *yalo-*
soup – *supu*
south – *sauca*
south wind – *ceva*
souvenir – *ivakananumi,*
suvania
speak – *vosa*
special – *drēdrē*
speed – *totolo*
spicy – *gaga, kati*
spider – *viritālawalawa*
spirit – *yalo-*
spoon – *itaki*
sport – *qito*
spring (season) – *vul-*
aitubutubu
square – *riririvi*
stairs – *ikabakaba*
stamp – (n) *sitaba,*
(v) *sitaba-taka,*
(with foot) *butu-ka*
stand – *tū* (cake)
standard – (n) *ivakarau,* (adj)
vakarautaki

star – *kalokalo*
start – *tekivū*
startled – *kidacala*
station – *sitēseni*
stay – *tiko*
steal – *butako-ca*
steam – *cawā*
step – *kālawa*
stick – (n) *kau, tabanikau,*
(v) *kabi,* (tr) *vākabira*
sting – (v) (wasp) *kati-a,*
(nettle) *coroga*
stomach – *kete-, wādumu*
stone – *vatu*
stop – (v) (action) *kua,*
mudu, (vehicle) *kele,*
(rain) *siga*
store – *sitoa*
storm – *draki cā*
story – *italanoa*
stove – *sitovu*
straight – *dodonu*
strange – *duatani*
stranger – *vūlagi*
street – *gaunisala*
strength – *kaukaua, igū*
string – *wā*
strong – *kaukaua, gūlevu*
student – *gonevuli*
stupid – *lialia, doce*
style – *icakacaka, imoimoi*

success, successful – (sports) *qāqā*, (fishing, hunting, business) *katoa*
sudden – *vakasaurī*
suffer – *kune rarawa*
sugar – *suka*
sugarcane – *dovu*
suit – *sutu*
summer – *vulaikatakata*
sun – *(matani)siga*
sunburn – *kafīsiga*
sunglasses – *matailoilo loaloa*
sunrise – *cabe na siga*
sunset – *dromu na siga*
supermarket – *supamākete*
sure – *kilā sara gā*
  make sure – *vakadeitaka*
surprised – *kurabui*
survive – *bula*
swear – *vosacā*
sweat – *buno*
sweet – (adj) *kamikamica*, (n) *loli*
sweet potato – *kumala*
swim – *qalo*, (go swimming in the sea) *sili waitui*

T

table – *tēveli*
tail – *bui-*
take – *taura*

talk – *vosa*
tall – *balavu*
tapa – *masi*
tapioca – *tavioka*
taro – *dalo*
tasteless – *drādranu, drādrāluka*
tasty – *kanavinaka, maleka*
tax – *ivakacavacava*
taxi – *teksi*
tea – *tī*
teacher – *qasenivuli*
teapot – *tīvote*
tear – (n) *wainimata-*, (v) *dresuka*
teaspoon – *itaki ni tī*
telegram – *telekaramu*
telephone – (n) *talevoni*, (v) *qiri*
television – *tīvī*
tell – *tukuna*
temperature – *(ivakarau ni) katakata*
tent – *valelaca*
test – *tovolea*
thank – *vakavinavinaka*
there – (where you are) *i keri*, (over there) *i keā*, (there is) *e dua*
thick – (solid) *vāvaku*, (liquid) *sosoko*

thief – *daubutako*
thin – (person) *lila*, (solid) *māmare*, (liquid) *waicala*
thing – *kā*
think – *nanuma, vākāsama, kilā beka*
 What do you think?
 A cava o nanuma?
 Keep quiet, I'm thinking.
 Tikolō, au vākāsama tiko.
 I think they've gone.
 Au kilā era sā lako beka.
third – *ikatolu*, (be third, come third) *katolu*
thirsty (to be) – *viagunu*
thought – *vākāsama*
thread – *wāniculacula*
throw – *viri-taka*
ticket – *tikite*
tide – *ua*, (low) *mati*
tidy – *maqosa*
tight – *qaco, tadrē*
time – *gauna*
tired (to be) – (exhausted) *oca*, (sleepy) *viamoce*
to – *i*, (person) *vei*, (in order to) *me*
toast – (n) *tosi, madrai tavu*, (v) *tavuna*
tobacco – *tavako*
today – *nikua*

together – *vata*
toilet – *valelailai*
toilet paper – *pepa nivalelailai*
tomato – *tōmata*
tomorrow – *nimataka*
tonight – *bogi nikua*
too – (excessive) *rui*, (also) *tale gā*
too much – *sīvia*
tooth – *bati-*
toothache – *mosi ni bati*
toothbrush – *barasi ni bati*
toothpaste – *wainimate ni bati*
top – *dela-, ulu-*
torch – (electric) *cina livaliva*
touch – (v) *tarā*
tour – *wāvoki, tua*
tourist – *saravanua, vūlagi saravanua*
toward – *i*
towel – *tauelu*
town – *tāuni*
track – *sala*, (footprints) *we-*
train – *sitīma (nivanua)*
translate – *vakadewa-taka*
tree – (generic) *vunikau*, (specific) *vu-*
 coconut tree – *vuniniu*

trip – *gādē*, (boat) *tirivu*
trouble – *leqa*
trousers – *tarausese*
truck – *lori*
true – *dina*
trust – *vakabauta, nuitaka*
try – (test) *tovolea*,
  (persevere) *sagā*
turn – *gole*, (tr) *vāgolea*,
  wirica
turn over – *vuki-ca*
turtle – *vonu*

U

ugly – *rairaicā*
ukulele – *ukalele*
umbrella – *iviu*
uncle –
  (father's elder brother)
  tama-levu,
  (father's younger brother)
  tama-lailai,
  (mother's brother) *mōmō*
uncomfortable –
  (person) *tiko vakacā*,
  (thing) *logalogacā*
under – *i ruku-*
understand – *macala*
  I understand.
  E macala vei au.

underwear – *isuluiloma*, (inf)
  sapo
unemployed – *tawacakacaka*
unhappy – *rarawa*
university – *univesitī*
unload – *tala-ca, vakasobu-ra*
unsafe – *rerevaki*
until – *me yacova*
up – *cake*
upstairs – *i cake*
use (v) – *vakayagataka*,
  (n) – *yaga*
useful – *yaga*

V

vacant – *lala*
vacation – (school holiday)
  sereki, (leave from work)
  livi, (trip) *gādē*
vaccination – *cula*
valley – *buca*
valuable – *yaga*
valuables – *iyau drēdrē*
value (price) – *isau*
vegetable – (root) *kākana
  dina*, (green) *kākana
  draudrau*
vegetarian – *tabu
  lewenimanumanu*
veil – *voela*
vendor – *volivolitaki*

very – *sara*
  very beautiful – *totoka sara*
view – (opinion) *rai*, (prospect) *irairai*
village – *koro*
vine – *vaini*
vinegar – *vinika*
vineyard – *loganivaini*
visit – (v) (to hospital, dormitory etc) *gādē*, (intr) *veisiko*, (tr) *sikova*
  Pay us a visit some time. *Bau gādē yani.*
visitor – *vūlagi*
  You have a visitor. *Dua nomu vūlagi.*
voice – *domo-*
vomit – *lua*
vote – *veidigidigī*

W

wait – *wāwā*, (tr) *wāraka*
waiter – *weita*
wake (someone) up – *vakayadrata*
walk – *taubale*
wall – (house) *lālaga*, (barrier) *bā*
want – *vinakata*

want to – *via*
war – *ivalu*
warm – *katakata toka*, *via katakata*
warn – *vakasala-taka*
wart – *somuna*
wash (clothes) – *savasava*, (tr) *savata*
wash hands – *vuluvulu*
wash (feet) – *sāsāvui*, (tr) *sāvuya*
watch – (v) *rai-ca*, (game, performance) *sarasara*, (tr) *sarava*, (n) *kaloko(niliga)*, *waji*
water – *wai*
waterfall – *savu*
watermelon – *mēleni*
way – *sala*
weak – *malumalumu*, *gōgō*
wealth – *iyau*
wealthy – *vutuniyau*
wear – *vaka-*
  wear a shirt – *vakasote*
weather – *draki*
weave – *talitali*, (tr) *tali-a*
wedding – *vakamau*, (traditional) *tevutevu*
week – *mācawa*
weigh – *vakarau-taka (na kena bībī)*

weight – *bībī*
welcome – *kidavaka*
well – (v) *vinaka*, (n) *toevu*
west – *rā*, *wesi*
west wind – *vuairā*
wet – *suasua*
whale's tooth – *tabua*
wheat – *witi*
whisper – *vakasolokakana*
white – *vulavula*
whole – *taucoko*
wide – *rāraba*, *rabalevu*
wife – *wati-* *(yalewa)*
wild (animal) – *kila*
win – *wini*
wind – *cagi*
window – *kātubaleka*
wine – *waini*
wing – *taba-*
winter – *vulaililiwa*
wire – *waya*
wireless – *wālesi*
wise – *yalomatua*
with – *(vata) kei*
within – *i loma ni*
without – *sega*
woman – *yalewa*
wonderful – *wānanavu*
wood – *kau*
wool – *kula*
word – *vosa*

work – (labour) *cakacaka*,
    (function properly) *vinaka*,
    mate, (effective) *mana*,
    (not working) *cā*, *mate*
world – *vuravura*
worm – *baca(niqele)*
worse – *torosobu*
worst – *cā duadua*, *imurimuri*
worth – *kena isau dina*
wound – *mavoa*
wrist – *ilabiniika*
write – *volavola*, (tr) *volā*
writing paper – *pepa ni*
    volavola
wrong – *cala*

Y

yam – *uvi*
year – *yabaki*
yellow – *dromodromo*
yes – *io*
yesterday – *nanoa*, *enanoa*
yet – (not yet) *se bera (ni)*
young – *gone*
youth – (young people)
    itabagone, (young man)
    cauravou

Z

zone – *yasayasa*

Emergencies

Help!	*Oilei!*
It's an emergency!	*Na leqa!*
There's been a road accident!	*Na coqa!*
Call a doctor!	*Qiria na vuniwai!*
Call an ambulance!	*Qiria na lori ni valenibula!*
Wave down a car!	*Tātaro motokā!*
I've been robbed!	*Butako!*
Call the police!	*Qiria na ovisa!*
My ... was stolen.	*E butakoci noqu ...*
I've been raped.	*Au sā kucuvi.*
Stop!	*Tū! (to vehicle) Kele!*
Go away!	*Lako tani!*
I'll call for the police!	*Au na kaciva na ovisa!*
Watch out!	*Qarauna!*
Thief!	*Butako!*
Fire!	*Kama!*
I've lost ...	*Sā yali ...*
my bags	*noqu iyāyā*
my money	*noqu ilavo*
my passport	*noqu pasipote*
I am ill.	*Au sā tauvimate.*
I am lost.	*Au sā sese.*
Where is the police station?	*I vei na sitēseni ni ovisa?*

Where are the toilets?	*I vei na valelailai?*
Could you help me please?	*Au kerea nomunī veivuke.*
Could I please use the telephone?	*Au vakayagataka mada na talevoni.*
I wish to contact my embassy/consulate.	*Au via qiri vuā na mata ni noqu matanitū.*
I speak Fijian.	*Au kilā na vosa vakaviti.*
I understand.	*Sā macala.*
I don't understand.	*Sega ni macala.*
I didn't realise I was doing anything wrong.	*Au sega ni kilā niu cala.*
I didn't do it.	*Au sega ni cakava.*
I'm sorry. I apologise.	*Isa, nī vosoti au sara.*

EMERGENCIES

Index